Sewing and Collecting
VINTAGE FASHIONS

Other books in the Creative Machine Arts Series, available from Chilton:

The Complete Book of Machine Embroidery, by Robbie and Tony Fanning
Creative Nurseries Illustrated, by Debra Terry and Juli Plooster
Creative Serging Illustrated, by Pati Palmer, Gail Brown and Sue Green
The Expectant Mother's Wardrobe Planner, by Rebecca Dumlao
The Fabric Lover's Scrapbook, by Margaret Dittman
Friendship Quilts by Hand and Machine, by Carolyn Vosburg Hall
Know Your Bernina, by Jackie Dodson
Know Your Sewing Machine, by Jackie Dodson
Pizzazz for Pennies, by Barb Forman

Sewing & Collecting
VINTAGE FASHIONS

Eileen MacIntosh

CHILTON COMPANY
Radnor, Pennsylvania

Designed by Culver Graphic Design

Manufactured in the United States of America
Cover photographs © 1988 by Lee Phillips; garments in cover photographs from the collection of
Sandy and Betty Ziebell, Mt. View, California.

Library of Congress Cataloging in Publication Data
MacIntosh, Eileen.
    Sewing and collecting vintage fashions.
    (Creative machine arts series)
    Bibliography: p. 165
    Includes index.
    1. Clothing and dress. 2. Clothing and dress —
Collectors and collection.   I. Title.   II. Title:
Vintage fashions.   III.   Series.
TT560.M32   1988   646'.47   87-47979
ISBN 0-8019-7799-1 (pbk.)

2 3 4 5 6 7 8 9 0   7 6 5 4 3 2 1 0

To LRH,

who's always there when I need
some just-plain-sensible advice—
and a laugh or two or three
when things get Too Serious!.

CONTENTS

FOREWORD

The last time I saw Eileen MacIntosh, she was all in white and looked like she'd just stepped off a stagecoach and into a western romance. Her white linen blouse sparkled, the high-button boots were shapely and a ribboned straw bonnet sat rakishly on her curls. What fun, I thought!

Fun, indeed . . .I didn't know how much until I read the manuscript of her book. Now I, like you, will poke my nose into many more boxes of interesting old clothes and, with a more knowledgeable eye, stroll through vintage clothing stores, looking for whatever catches my eye. And always examining the seams, of course! (You'll know what I mean when you get to that part, and will also learn when sewing machines came to be popular.)

Sewing and Collecting Vintage Fashions is a beginner's manual, and will introduce you to a lively new world you may never have considered exploring. It was perfect reading for someone like me, who likes to look romantic, even historical, when "dressed up," but didn't know all the options available. If you're a novice, too, Eileen presents the information you need to start putting more authentic vintage into your daily dress, not just once a year at a costume ball or for Halloween.

Eileen's resource sections will help you track down anything you need for sewing vintage fashions — or buying readymades. She lists addresses for everything from Civil War buttons to specialty auctions.

I'm not handy with a needle, but the pattern selections available are impressive enough to make me find a good dressmaker. And I can't thank Eileen enough for writing about the care of fabrics. When all else fails, I'm going to put my stained white garments on fresh snow, as advised, and watch the sun bleach them back to perfection. The chapter on fabrics is worth the price of the book alone. You will now understand how to care for ordinary as well as fragile fabrics, and you'll certainly be hip to polyester forever. Breathes there a woman who hasn't sweated in a polyester blouse and wondered why?

Romance author Heather Graham helped her husband to create a Victorian evening suit that passes very fashionably when other gentlemen are in black tie. Dennis is an avid reader and collector of Victoriana and he's pleased as punch to wear it: "A little like actually living there," he says wistfully. So go ahead, make it happen. Who wants mini dresses when you can sweep the stairs in velvet or linen? Life is short, and if you prefer another century, indulge yourself.

Life is so mundane today. As Barbara Cartland says, "Too many women wear beige and look like potatoes. A woman needs some color in her life, and if you aren't a little bit gaudy no one notices you."

I'm not suggesting you take on pink and diamonds á la Cartland but, as Miss Gooch in "Mame" says, "live, live, live." Be more daring.

I recently came across a Bea Lilly beanie in a New York thrift shop. It's pink satin and bejeweled and looks great with a black evening dress and my antique fur muff. I once attended Lord and Lady Bath's jumble sale (even the aristocracy get rid of junk) and found a Victorian parasol that needed only slight repairs. A friend of mine, at an estate sale, just bought two beautiful European fans. Another friend has started looking for beaded purses from the last century. Vintage fashions and accessories will get you, too, once you open your mind to mixing the old and the new in everyday wear.

My newfound interest in vintage fashion is all due to Eileen. I'll never be able to pass up a box of interesting old clothing again. I'll always wonder what I might have missed!

Kathryn Falk, Publisher
Romantic Times magazines and books

PREFACE

History? B-o-r-i-n-g! At least, that's what *I* thought. And "costumes" were what I hastily improvised for my kids, an hour before trick-or-treating on Halloween. Then I started collecting quilts.

To restore my antique quilts, I shopped at rummage sales and auctions for old (and I mean *old*) clothing. In my opinion, a brand new patch on a hundred-year-old quilt looks ridiculous. However, in some cases, I bought vintage clothes that were too nice to cut up. So I saved them. Even wore them now and then.

They were fun to wear. People complimented me and were interested in the old fabrics and styles. I've always been a romantic and I became interested in the lives of the women who wore these fashions. Above all, I liked the clothing and I wanted more for my wardrobe.

The next step was buying wearable vintage clothing in slightly damaged condition, which meant searching for materials to repair them. Boxes of antique buttons. Spools of old thread. Scraps of lace. My sewing room was now my studio and it had that distinctive, musty smell of other people's attics. Suddenly I was wearing more antique clothing, even lecturing to historical groups on Victorian fashions.

In time, I supplemented my antique clothing with reproductions. Some were purchased ready-made. I made others from historic patterns. A tea stain on a Victorian blouse is heartbreaking; a tea stain on a reproduction simply means that I haul out the bleach. A new world opened up, as I discovered historical patterns and suppliers of the "correct" sewing materials. And Victorian patterns led to Colonial, to Medieval, and to eras in between.

Next came the excuses to wear all these clothes. I joined several organizations that were involved with living history. On April 19th of each year, I'd wake the family at 5:00 am for the reenactment of the Revolutionary battle on Lexington Green and the later fight in Concord. During the summers, we volunteered at Minute Man National Park, where we explained our Colonial clothing to the tourists. As a family, we became fascinated with history.

Even my contemporary wardrobe took on a vintage look. My turn-of-the-century Chinese jacket was worn with a leotard and black slacks. An embroidered shawl from the 1920s added elegance to a basic dinner dress. My 1890s white cotton blouse looked terrific over a camisole, combined with blue jeans. I found great excuses to add little vintage touches to my ensembles. At the very least, I'd wrap some antique lace around my ponytail.

Finally, I started a newsletter for those of us who admire historical clothing. It was a labor of love, and gave me an excuse to learn more and more about this fascinating field. Now I'm hooked on vintage fashions. They are a part of my daily life, and I'm happy to share my interests through this book. It contains the most important things I've learned in the last several years. It is intended as a guide and reference book for people interested in historical clothing. Whether you are involved in living history; need a quick costume for a party; are an old-time car, bicycle, or train buff; attend murder mystery parties; or simply long for those eras of lost elegance, you'll learn valuable information in this book. There's even a chapter for writers, who also need accurate clothing information.

This book will get you started if you're a beginner. It will prevent expensive and heartbreaking errors. For more experienced collectors and history buffs, you'll find some fresh ideas and ways to enjoy your hobby more. No matter what your level of expertise, the resources and references in the back of the book will be valuable. Historical clothing has been both fun and educational; I hope my enthusiasm is infectious.

ACKNOWLEDGMENTS

Thanks to the many people who helped this book become a reality:

Robbie, who started with a dream and patiently guided it to completion. Kathy, one of the world's funniest, most positive-thinking editors. Kathryn Falk and the RT staff, who provided a constant supply of witty advice, as well as valuable material for the book. Debbie Deutsch and Meryl W., who shared auction-ing expertise and plenty of giggles. The entire, wonderful Bradley family and staff of JB's. My personal "cheerleaders": Bjo, Bobby Ann, Claire, Diana H., Jane Pierce, Joe & Lindy, Larry & Sheila, Linda Stuart, Kia, Lloyd Carl, Martha Wells, Pam McCampbell, Pat Brusch, Pat Werner, Robert Schwartz, Roger Mulford, my-brother-Bruce, Muriel, Len & Kathy, Ruth, and the MacIntoshes. And the people whose suggestions, references, projects, and humor were so vital in completing this book: Elyse, Colleen, Randy, Ray, Leif, Sheryl J., and the entire staffs of the public libraries of Belmont, Massachusetts, and Dunedin, Florida.

Very special thanks to the many other wonderful people who've contributed to this book, especially to Saundra Ros Altman, Janet Burgess, Debbie & Molly of Molly's/Grandmother's, Harriet Engler, Bobby Ann Loper, Heidi Marsh, Diana Venegas and staff, Jenny Reily, Jim Garrett, Alan & Alexa Robinson, the staff at Folkwear, Turner Enterprises, and the Aardvarks.

And an *enormous* thank you (which really isn't enough) to my husband and children, who not only patiently understand my needs as an artist/writer, but also encourage me in all that I do.

CHAPTER 1

How to Get Started

Old-fashioned clothing. The styles — the *flair* — of the past. They add such color to history, and they can add color to your wardrobe.

In this book, you'll learn about fashions of the past, and the times that created them. You'll learn what clothing looked like. Not just plain old drawings, but descriptions of the fabrics and colors that were popular. How people walked and sat in these clothes, due to manners or the structure of the clothing itself.

You'll learn how to create these same clothes at home. Or purchase readymade reproduction clothing from your favorite fashion eras. You'll even discover the secrets of successfully buying antique and vintage clothing.

You'll also learn shortcuts in case you need a hasty costume. Even non-sewers can create spectacular outfits with these tips. Of course, you'll also want to read the chapter on creating accurate clothing of the past, so you'll know which details you're skipping with the shortcuts.

And you'll find ideas on how to include old-fashioned styles in your everyday wardrobe, for a personal fashion statement that has nothing to do with wearing a costume.

Elan MacIntosh in a Victorian day dress of fine cotton, banded with ribbon. Dress from the collection of Barbara Temperley; used by permission.

Many references and resources are listed in the back of the book. You can find everything you'll need, in these books and catalogues you can order by mail. You'll even learn about clubs and organizations in your area, filled with other people like you, who enjoy history and old-fashioned clothing.

I've filled my book with ideas and tips that you can use right away, no matter *what* your interest in clothing of the past.

Your fashion adventure is about to begin. . . .

QUESTIONS TO ANSWER BEFORE YOU BEGIN

Fig. 1–1

Whether you want a costume for your child's Halloween party, an Edwardian-looking blouse for the office, or your own authentic Victorian ball gown, you'll need to think about a few things before plunging ahead.

Which era will you choose?

There are two ways to approach historical clothing: Some of you have a general picture of a costume in your mind, but you don't know exactly when it was popular; someone else may have an invitation to a 1930s party, and not know quite what they were wearing back then. Chapter 2 will help to identify the fashions you want. It covers the most distinctive styles, along with interesting allied information on the years when they were popular.

How accurate does it have to be?

Fig. 1–2

If it's a one-time, fun costume for a party, you may not care how realistic it is. I've outlined shortcuts in Chapter 4, when accuracy is less important than meeting a deadline.

On the other hand, if you're planning the ultimate, perfect representation of an era for a living history exhibit, you'll be more interested in Chapters 6, 7, and 8 on authentic reproductions. And the References and Resources listings will give you mail-order sources for everything from boots to sewing supplies, no matter what your needs.

Do you want to sew all or part of your costume?

Beginners can use very easy historical patterns. In fact, everyday clothes were often simple, since patterns were not commercially available until the nineteenth century. Women made up their own patterns. Homemade gowns included many improvised details.

Of course, a simple pattern isn't always quick or easy. In some cases, you'll add new terms to your vocabulary, because clothing pieces had special names that are no longer used. You may be confused making an 1890s blouse, when the pattern keeps calling it a *waist*, the word for blouse until the early 1900s. Or you may have a little diamond-shaped piece for the underarm that you have to fit by trial-and-error.

Fig. 1–3

Some of the better historical patterns, especially for the late nineteenth and early twentieth centuries, have about a *zillion* pieces and *volumes* of instructions. Okay, I'm exaggerating. But you may be completely overwhelmed when you open the envelope, and it's easy to give up halfway through cutting out those zillions of pieces. I have good news for you: Once you have the pieces cut out, the hardest work is done. It is still time consuming to complete the sewing, but it doesn't take any special genius. That's why they include such amazing pattern directions — so that those of us who are all thumbs can actually sew up the item without doing anything stupid. I speak from long experience. I'm one of those people who follows the directions *only* if all else fails. But when I sew one of these multipart patterns, I am forced to read the directions and follow them carefully. The more complex the pattern, the easier the instructions seem to be. I can do the sewing after a hectic day, when I wouldn't tackle anything as complex as making buttered toast!

Sewing historical patterns is similar to sewing contemporary patterns. If you can't handle the tailoring on a basic modern jacket pattern, don't try a Civil War cloak with braid and tassels and sequins and who-knows-what-else.

Special Note: Never give up on historical patterns. If you find that you can't deal with sewing, select a pattern you love, buy the fabric, and hand the whole thing to a dressmaker. Or do some of the work yourself, and have a dressmaker (or a relative who sews?) do the rest. Or try as much cutting out and sewing as you can handle, and then turn it over to a pro. If you want something unique, your best choice may be a historical pattern. All these possibilities and more are covered in Chapter 3.

If you don't sew at all, and don't want to, there are abundant sources of custom-made historical clothing. You may be surprised to find that many, *many* people in this country wear old-fashioned clothes, for one reason or another. Living history re-enactors, old-time car enthusiasts, and even people who attend murder mystery parties, are looking for historical clothing. We'll talk about these options in Chapter 6.

How much do you want to spend?

The bargain-priced cotton blouse may not be such a bargain after all. And the gorgeous, permanent-press fabric for your gown may be an expensive disaster, if you don't know the tips you'll learn here. Read this entire book before you invest much money in clothing. The advice on selecting fabric for sewing will also apply to buying ready-made fashions. And the things to look for in ready-made purchases will prevent similar mistakes when you're sewing for yourself. Of course, if you don't have time to read the whole book before you splurge on the goodies for a costume, read as much as possible in the chapters that apply to you. You'll learn enough to prevent the worst disasters.

Will you wear antique clothing?

Read Chapter 8 before you spend a king's ransom on a traffic-stopping gown that will be in shreds two days later. Some clothing problems, such as certain stains, can be repaired. Other, less visible, damage can make a garment unwearable. Age is often a factor here. For example, if you want to wear an authentic Civil War ball gown, you'll have to settle for an authentic reproduction of a Civil War ball gown. Why? Nearly all silk from that era is so old that it is ready to tear or shred when you wear it. If you have the good fortune to find a wearable silk gown from that era, it belongs in a museum.

In Chapter 8 you'll learn which "real" antique clothing to avoid—and which to grab. I've seen women buy magnificent silk Victorian gowns with a tear here and there, not realizing that the gowns were ready to disintegrate. And I've bought antique textiles (including clothing) at ridiculously low prices, because I can re-move many hideous stains that scare away other customers. There

Fig. 1–4

are no guarantees in antique and vintage clothing, but a few shopping tips will help prevent disappointing mistakes. Chapter 8 covers those tips.

How do you care for your new "old" wardrobe?

You'll read about safely repairing, storing and cleaning textiles in your growing collection in Chapter 8. Let me say right now, you should *not* keep your antique Worth gown in an airtight plastic bag. Fabrics need to b-r-e-a-t-h-e! Storing gowns in plastic bags, "because they'll keep the dust and bugs out," has probably done as much damage as moths and silverfish combined. I've seen too many wonderful textiles destroyed by well-meaning individuals who wrapped them in plastic.

How do you choose accurate colors?

If you're fed up with flourescent-colored clothes, you're ready for some softer, more flattering additions to your everyday wardrobe. Chapter 9 will give you fun ideas and a new perspective on what you wear to work. Office clothing doesn't have to be so ho-hum, after all.

If you're a writer, particularly a romance writer, you may be tempted to skip right to the chapter that lists reference materials. Don't! Chapter 10 will tell you why you need to do more than just look at pictures. Artists and illustrators will pick up some pointers here, too.

What if you fall in love with historical clothing?

If you need an excuse to sew, collect, and/or wear historical clothing, check the listing of Clubs, Organizations, Periodicals. There are groups specializing in every era, and some groups that cover several eras just for the fun of wearing different costumes. (And their members are perfectly normal people, just like you and me. I freely admit to being a bit eccentric in my love of clothing from the past. However, I'm also active in my church, I am a Girl Scout leader, and live a fairly average life. Most other clothing enthusiasts are equally "normal," and you'll discover long-lasting friendships among them).

Vintage fashions are wonderful, no matter what your interest. And reading this book is going to make fashion a lot more fun!

Fig. 1–5

CHAPTER 2

Finding Your Era

*Y*ou're ready to start, but you don't know what "your" era looks like? Or you have a picture in your mind, perhaps of a woman wearing huge balloon sleeves, and you're not sure when that was popular. (Check early Victorian years and the 1890s for those particular sleeves.) Or you want a wonderful historical costume which will emphasize your tiny waist or minimize chubby arms. Or maybe the invitation says "Sherlock Holmes Party," and the fashions are a mystery to you!

If you already have a visual effect in mind but don't know its era, browse through the illustrations in this chapter and see if you find what you want. Then you can read the descriptions for more details. If you're starting with a time period, read about earlier fashions to get a feeling for what came right before "your" era. Not every aspect of clothing of every time period is shown here (that would be a series of books in itself); this chapter will help you zero in on the correct time. Check your library and some of the books listed under References for the complete story on the clothing you have in mind.

Meanwhile, here's a very rough, era-by-era description of the most popular historical periods for costuming. I've added histori-

Vivien Leigh as Scarlett O'Hara, in Gone With the Wind. Copyright © 1939 Selznick International Pictures, Inc.; Ren. 1967 Metro-Goldwyn-Mayer, Inc.

Fig. 2-1

cal notes to give the times a bit more color for you. The Middle Ages weren't really so primitive, once you realize all their inventions. People weren't so interested in comfort, which shows up in the clothing of the early Middle Ages.

MEDIEVAL TIMES

Also called the Middle Ages, the Medieval period extended from about A.D. 476 to A.D. 1450. My dictionary tells me that the "Dark Ages" were from A.D. 476 to the end of the tenth century. But they weren't so dark. During the fifth century, people were looking for ways to change lead into gold. (Think in terms of sword-and-sorcery movies.) King Arthur lived in the sixth century. Check the history books listed in the References section for very early Medieval clothing; most fashion references begin with 1066. However, fashions didn't change too rapidly during the earliest years, which makes research easy. Your best references will be art of the time, at the locale that you have in mind. Also check the listing of clubs, especially the Society for Creative Anachronism.

By 1066, cotton had been used in Arab countries for over 400 years. Linen and wool had been manufactured for over 100 years. London Bridge had been built. In 1066, William I was crowned King of England on Christmas Day, and Halley's Comet was first seen.

My descriptions are for English clothing. If you have a particular area in mind, use this information to get started, then research your own time or place. Communication and travel were limited, so styles were often specific for each locale, without influence from other areas. Of course, clothing technology was fairly limited then, so certain fashion elements will be common throughout the world.

Linen was *the* fabric in 1066, with wool a close second. Silk was used on the most formal occasions. Colors came from vegetable dyes, so there were many warm colors, and few blues and greens. (Indigo became popular later. Until it was easily imported from India, indigo blue was rare and valuable.) Check with your needlework shop for color cards of naturally dyed yarns. These will

Fig. 2–2

Fig. 2–3

give you an idea of the range available until the middle of the nineteenth century, when new dyes were created.

Men wore trousers (like loose, thick tights), leather shoes, an under-tunic and an over-tunic, both usually knee length (Fig. 2–1). A simple fabric or leather belt kept the tunics in place. A man wore a cloak; it was basically a rectangular or semi-circular piece of fabric. The cloak was tied, or held in place with a brooch or ring. Sometimes men wore swords and/or daggers, carried spears, and other military hardware.

Women wore similar tunics, but longer (Fig. 2–2). The under-tunic reached the ground, and had long, close-fitting sleeves. The over-tunic was briefer, often knee length with shorter, flared sleeves. Women sometimes wore belts. They concealed their hair under large, heavy veils, usually white linen. Women also wore cloaks, similar to the ones for men, which were draped gracefully and held in place with brooches. The most common necklines were V-necks and simple round necks with a center opening. Think in very simple terms. For decoration, they used an embroidered hemline or a specially woven decorative band. Keep in mind that these were heavy clothes, and draping was necessary to balance the weight. For example, longer veils draped over the arms, so that the head and neck wouldn't be under such stress.

By the twelfth century, veils were sometimes smaller, or not worn at all, to show braided or plaited hair. Bodices were more fitted. Sleeves became exaggerated so they trailed, sometimes reaching the floor (Fig. 2–3). Belts were more decorative, and were sometimes worn quite low. Men started wearing beards and moustaches, and could have shoulder-length hair. Their hemlines were higher, too, showing more leg! Think in terms of Robin Hood for this era. Jewelry became more popular and refined, hair styles and headdresses were more ornate and creative, and leather was used for more outerwear. Fur-lined cloaks were worn. Jewels were used for decoration. Pleats were sewn into skirts, under-gowns and sleeves. There was more variety to the weave and fiber of fabrics. Blues became fashionable when indigo was imported from India. Fashions were more flattering than in previous years.

St. Bartholomew's Hospital was founded in England during this era. Troubador music became popular throughout France. Arabs were manufacturing paper in Spain. Chess was first played in

9

Finding Your Era

Fig. 2–4

England. Thomas à Becket became Archbishop of Canterbury. Glass windows were used in England, in place of oiled paper, but few windows actually opened. Homes were not comfortable, with plain benches and stools for seating. Fireplaces were smoky and gave little heat. Candles and oil lamps were expensive to use, so most people went to bed early at night. Horse racing became a sport. People were still more interested in what they were *doing* than in how comfortable their lives were. Survival was still the most important factor, since life held many environmental dangers. Food was not plentiful. When gathering food, there was still a good likelihood of being attacked by a wild animal. And there were few ways to preserve the food once it was brought home. When you're talking in those terms, it's easy to see that having comfortable furniture or flattering clothing is far down on the list of priorities.

By the thirteenth and fourteenth centuries, clothing was more fitted and decorated. Life was becoming a little easier. Linen was being manufactured in England. Sleeveless over-gowns with open sides and deep armholes became fashionable. Shoes with long pointy toes were worn in court (think of court jesters). They sometimes wore hoods that extended into long points. Men were wearing very short skirts with long woolen stockings (Fig. 2–4), while women's gowns were gaining trains. By now, cotton was being manufactured in Spain.

In this era, Francis of Assisi established the Franciscan friars. The Magna Carta was sealed. Genghis Khan was conquering his part of the world. Tiles replaced wood and thatch on London roofs. Newgate Prison was founded. The Inquisition forbade laymen to read the Bible. Eyeglasses were invented, as were the mechanical clock, the suction pump, and the windmill. Crop rotation increased the food supply tremendously. Communities became interdependent. It was no longer "every man for himself," and this improved the quality of life for all. Among the upper classes, this meant leisure time was available.

At the close of the Medieval era, women's gowns had high waists. Women sometimes wore their hair loose, and headdresses were dramatically stylized. This is when those hats with single or double "horns" on them (not like animals' horns—we're talking about the ones you picture on a princess) were coming into style. Other hats were heavily decorated with trim, beads, braid, and

Fig. 2–5

jewels (Fig. 2–5). The most fashionable fabrics for court were velvets and silks, and many had all-over patterns. Women wore necklaces of beads or heavy jewels. Engagement rings became fashionable. Sleeves were sometimes gathered at the wrist, and low, wide necklines were popular. Some men wore boots and heavy, pleated over tunics. Their hats were also decorative.

THE RENAISSANCE

The Renaissance extended from the fourteenth through sixteenth centuries, so there is a slight overlap with what is termed the Middle Ages.

In the fifteenth century, Christopher Columbus was born and discovered (or rediscovered) America. The Gutenberg Press printed the Bible. Bowling-like sports became illegal in England, and golf and fute-ball were discouraged in Scotland. Hans Holbein, Durer, Botticelli, Michelangelo, and Leonardo da Vinci were creating their masterpieces—and da Vinci invented the parachute. Copernicus was studying the stars. Richard III became King of England. Life was becoming more interesting and more social, with less emphasis upon merely surviving.

Clothing was still similar to that of the Medieval era, but more ornate and fitted. Women's sleeves ranged from tight and fitted, to flared with wide, decorated, stiffened cuffs. The sleeves no longer trailed on the ground. Skirts were wide, bodices were form-fitting, and waistlines were more natural. Square necklines were most popular, and hoods became fashionable. Here is where we see the "gabled" hood and veil (Fig. 2–6).

Fig. 2–6

Men's tunics still varied in length, but we begin to see shirts appearing, with doublets. Sleeves were fitted, flared, or gathered. Shoes were round-toed, with a strap over the instep. (Similar to ballet slippers, but in more basic materials.) Some were made from velvet or other decorative fabric, though leather remained popular for daily wear. Ankle boots were also worn. Large feathers decorated hats, which ranged from small and soft-crowned to wide-brimmed. Chains and pendants were worn for decoration. Hose were now made of silk and velvet, as well as the traditional wool.

Fig. 2–7

In the sixteenth century, pocket handkerchiefs were in use. Black-lead pencils were manufactured in England. The process of manufacturing mirrors was greatly improved. Henry VIII ruled England, as did Elizabeth I in later years. Raphael, El Greco, and Titian were popular artists. Improved trade routes made spices more available and Italian cooking became popular throughout Europe. Pineapples, coffee, turkey, tobacco, and chocolate were imported to Europe. Slaves were brought to American colonies by Spain. Spinning wheels were readily available. Sealing wax sealed letters. People played card games, cricket and billiards. Horse-drawn coaches became fashionable. Shakespeare, Donne, and Jonson were born and began writing in this century. An earthquake in London in 1580 shook its approximately 180,000 citizens.

In women's clothing of the early 1500s, corselets restricted the bust, ribcage, and waist. The bodice of the gown was as flat as possible, and tight upper sleeves restricted movement (Fig. 2–7). Back and/or front lacing of gowns revealed decorative undergowns. Slashing, held together with jewels and heavy embroidery, was also used to reveal undergarments. Quilted undergarments were both decorative and practical; they kept women warm in those pre-central-heating days. Drop earrings and pearls became popular. The large, square necklines were sometimes filled in with linen, often in frills.

Men's clothing was clearly influenced by Henry VIII's voluminous garments (Fig. 2–8). Fur trimmed, slashed sleeves were full and padded. Enormous coats with fur linings added to the illusion of size. Men's fashionable accessories included chain belts, codpieces, and slashed or embroidered shoes.

After Henry VIII, women's fashions developed predictably. Sleeves became voluminous, often padded or stuffed to remain full (Fig. 2–9). Pearl-studded fabrics and embroidered laces were among the decorations used for fabric. Necklines were more often filled in (Fig. 2–10). Ruffs became fashionable on collars and cuffs, but not so exaggerated as during the later reign of Elizabeth I. Men's fashions remained ornate after Henry VIII, but not quite so gaudy and full (Fig. 2–11). Jerkins had padded chests, but were far more figure revealing than the previous styles.

In researching costume, it sometimes helps to think of movies. Obviously, movies related to Henry VIII and Elizabeth I are helpful, as are those about Christopher Columbus. Pirates and pri-

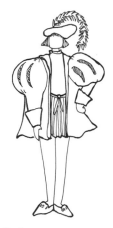

Fig. 2–8

Fig. 2–9

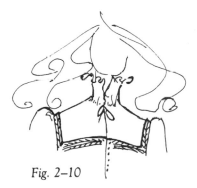

Fig. 2–10

Fig. 2–11

vateers were on the high seas, many of them licensed by Elizabeth I, though not all pirate movies represent that era, and not many are accurately costumed! Shakespearean plays are more useful references.

"Good Queen Bess, she smiled at me!" Worshipped by her people, Elizabeth I returned their love in full measure. Each day at the Renaissance Pleasure Faire, weekends from April 26 to June 1 in Agoura, California, the queen visits the festivities, welcoming spring and greeting peasant, noble and 20th century visitor alike. Photo used by permission of Globe Photos, Inc.

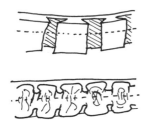

Fig. 2–12

Fig. 2–13

AMERICAN COLONIAL

By the arrival of the eighteenth century, cotton had been manufactured in England for over 50 years. The Russian fur trade was well established. Income and property taxes were standardized in England, and postal service permitted rapid communications. Newspapers had ads, ice cream was a fashionable dessert, and tea and coffee were common beverages. Stockings and fountain pens were manufactured in France, starting in 1657. Water closets were no longer a novelty. A watch now had a minute hand. Cheques were used as currency. Plate glass was available. Huge weaving mills produced fabric. England had a tax on windows, Russia had one on beards, and Berlin had one on unmarried women. Early in the eighteenth century, an English inventor developed carriage springs, which made travel far more comfortable. Dick Turpin and fellow highwaymen haunted the roadsides to take advantage of this increase in carriage travel. In 1731, a law was passed to forbid English factory workers from emigrating to America.

In women's fashions, we still see the flattened chest from the fifthteenth and sixteenth centuries, and necklines were frequently squared. However, decorations were more flattering and feminine, as opposed to the gaudy and ornate trim of earlier centuries. In the mid-eighteenth century, upper-class women decorated their gowns with ribbons, silk, lace, and ruching—a kind of gathering (Fig. 2–12). Pastel colors were fashionable. Women wore a hooped underskirt, often as large as 8 yards in circumference. Wide, full skirts were supported by undergarment structures called *panniers* or "side buckets," which looked like two huge, round baskets held on a belt so that they rested on the sides of the hips. The profile was fairly flat, but the sack-backed gown (also called a "sacque") draped to cover the corset protrusions, and gave a fuller profile than other styles. In some areas, a bum roll (Fig. 2–13) enlarged the hips in profile, but not enough to balance the exaggerated style of the panniers. Wealthier women had collapsible hoopskirts so that they could fit through doorways. This is the era of the white-powdered hairstyles, and patches worn as beauty marks. Heavy, elaborate hairstyles made head movement difficult if not hazardous!

Women in the Colonies did not necessarily dress as their wealthy, English counterparts did. If you worked on a farm, it is

Fig. 2–14

Fig. 2–15

Fig. 2–16

safe to say that powdered wigs and panniers were out of the question. Colors were darker and fabrics more practical than the pastel silks of English society. With the approach of the Revolution, many American women deliberately broke the laws in order to weave and dye their own fabrics at home. This may have imparted a more rustic appearance to the clothing, but it also made a political statement. Weaving rapidly improved in America, and Martha Washington proudly wore silk at George's Inauguration. One of the most common errors in Colonial costuming is to assume that eighteenth-century muslin was the same as our muslin today. Muslin in the 1700s was a very fine grade of cotton, similar in smoothness to fine Egyptian cotton. It was also pure white; only workmen and the lower classes wore the more practical unbleached fabrics. The muslin might be printed with a design, or embroidered with sprigs of flowers. Colonial clothing also differed widely from one area to the next. See the References section for books which will tell you the details of the time and locale you're representing.

Under her gown, a woman wore a chemise-like garment. It was usually made of white muslin, and most resembled a traditional nightgown (Fig. 2–14). It could be plain or ruffled. If ruffled, this might show above the neckline of the gown. This chemise plus an underskirt was called "undress." The underskirt served as a petticoat in some cases, and often was expected to be seen. It might be a color that complemented the gown, or it might be embroidered. Undress was where a woman could reveal her sewing skills. For example, a woman wore "pockets," which were purses that tied around the waist (Fig. 2–15). The pocket was sometimes decorated with ornate embroidery, and a single woman wore her pocket over her underskirt, to be seen by eligible bachelors. It showed an interested man that she had skill in sewing. A married woman wore her pocket under her underskirt, and reached it through a concealed opening.

Women might wear cloth slippers, but for practical wear in the Colonies, leather shoes were more common. As with men's shoes, there were no "right" and "left" shoes. People alternated which foot they wore a shoe on, so that the shoes wore out evenly.

Women did not reveal their elbows, as a matter of propriety. They covered their heads with a small cap such as a *mob cap*, or a small bit of lace for decoration (Fig. 2–16). The cap remained on whether indoors or out, and was worn underneath a hat when a woman chose to wear one outdoors (Fig. 2–17).

Keep in mind that British goods were not purchased during the Revolution. They may have been seized as part of the loot when a British trade ship was taken, but that is the only way new British-made clothing found its way to the Patriots. As a result, women were dressing in old clothes from pre-war years. If they had to work while their men were in battle, the clothes might become

Fig. 2–17

Mrs. Campbell plays the piano in her parlor at Prairietown. Photo courtesy of Conner Prairie.

Finding Your Era

Fig. 2–18

shabby with wear. By the time the war was over, even the "Sunday best" gowns were probably put into daily service, just to have something to wear.

During the Colonial era, most men wore fitted breeches with a loose-fitting shirt of fine muslin. Footwear included knee socks and leather shoes or boots. A cutaway coat or long overcoat was common outerwear (Fig. 2–18). At the neck, a man might wear a scarf tied as a cravat or in a bow. The more practical neckwear of the average man was a thin band of linen. This band, a couple of inches wide and a couple of yard long, was looped around the neck for decoration, and doubled as a sling to carry heavy objects, or as a bandage in case of an accident. A vest was also frequently worn, at all class levels. Men's breeches did not have belts or fly fronts. Breeches fitted well with a drop front and buttons toward the hip bones, and often buckled at the knee for a precise fit. Long pants were not usual, and were still considered to be Irish garb. When planning Colonial men's clothing, think of Benjamin Franklin, George Washington, and Paul Revere. This was the era of the tricorn, a three-cornered hat.

One of my favorite movies for clothing of this era is *Revolution* with Al Pacino. There are some details that I question, but it generally conveys a far more sensible impression of everyday fashions than most movies about that time period. Our nation wasn't filled with men wearing perfectly white, starched shirts! This movie is particularly graphic and fairly depressing, so I don't recommend it for your children.

THE REGENCY

The Regency is considered to be from 1811–1820 in England. After the American Revolutionary War, many events had changed the way people lived and dressed.

After its own Revolution, France set many fashionable trends. Lightweight, movable furniture was a novelty, made possible with mahogany imported from Santo Domingo and the Bahamas. The fashions of France, from dampened gowns to ornate silk bonnets, were brought to England with varying degrees of popularity.

Fig. 2–19

"The Beau," George Brummel, lived from 1778–1840, and had the most profound influence on men's clothing from that era forward. He had three tailors, one each for his breeches, his coats, and his waistcoats! Despite his humble background, he was proof that any well-dressed, well-mannered man could successfully mingle with the upper classes. He also helped popularize frequent bathing, for which countless noses were probably grateful.

Appearances in society had a major effect on fashion. Parties, balls, and walks in the park dictated distinctive clothing for each purpose. The streets of London were lit with gaslights, so travel to evening entertainment became safer and more popular. By 1813, the waltz became the popular, romantic dance, changing skirts on ball gowns to a fuller design. By 1818, the Atlantic Ocean could be crossed in less than a month, encouraging an exchange of visitors, ideas, and fashions.

Women's dresses were generally high-waisted (today called "empire" style). The waist reached its highest in 1815, coinciding with the longest sleeves, which covered the back of the hand. This is also the year when metal hooks were introduced as concealed fastenings in clothes. Some ladies were smart enough to use them as early as 1760 with concealed eyelets, but this was primarily for outerwear, as the hooks and eyelets were large. (Metal eyelets were actually patented in 1823.) Other closures included worked eyelets on either side, laced together; buttons on either side, laced in a similar fashion; buckles; buttons and buttonholes; or visible metal hooks. Sleeves were sometimes puffed at the shoulder, with a long, fitted undersleeve and an optional ruffle at the wrist (Fig. 2–19). Toward the end of the Regency, a low-cut bodice became more modest with a *chemisette* underneath (which you can think of as an elegant dickey). That is, it was a decorative, sleeveless garment which filled in the neck and upper chest areas, to look like a blouse underneath the gown. Skirts were flat in front, flared to the side, and gathered in back. Armholes were cut to fit precisely, allowing little movement.

Fabrics included wool, muslin, soft silk, and perhaps a calico. (*Calico* derives from *Calcutta cloth*, in reference to its Indian origins. Think about the colors and smaller prints available from India today.) Early in the Regency, white was the preferred color for gowns. The influence was from classical marble statues, which were, of course, white. Soft and light colors were coming into fash-

Fig. 2–20

Fig. 2–21

ion, as were cambric, poplin and muslin. (Muslin was still a high-quality cotton.) The fabric might be embroidered (especially muslin), printed in stripes, or decorated with dots or a small repeat pattern. The edges of the gown could be bordered with an ivy or honeysuckle design. Gowns were sometimes quite plain, but many were adorned with puffs, bows, lace, ruffles, rosettes, fabric-covered buttons, and so on. Colorful trim was popular, to add distinction to the uniform appearance of the common white gown.

Under her gown, a woman might wear a corset. In the early nineteenth century, corsets were used to restrain the shape; enhancing the figure was simply a side benefit. Clothes fit precisely, and an extra quarter-inch of fat could tear the garment. Thus, a chemise might be enough for a slender miss, while someone whose weight varied from week to week needed her figure kept a constant size by artificial means. Padding the breasts was losing popularity, but some probably continued this practice. A "bum roll," a cotton ball (like a small pillow), or a little bustle supported the back of the skirt and added volume. Drawers (*very* rarely worn) consisted of two separate "legs," attached to a waistband. Stockings were generally flesh-colored or white. Undergarments were not worn unless necessary. The idea was to reveal the figure as much as possible, through the gown. Shoes were similar to flat slippers or half-boots, though some women wore boots up to the knee. Leather was used for boots, as was linen in the summer. The popular slippers were so simple to make that shoemaking became an acceptable hobby for women of leisure. Overshoes were worn for protection outdoors, and they were fashioned to match the slippers.

Outerwear might include a large shawl (an elegant Paisley or Kashmir, or a cheap imitation), a Spencer (a short jacket, cut similar to the bodice of the gown), turbans, bonnets (Fig. 2–20), fans, tall stick parasols, and short gloves. Eighteenth century pockets were replaced by reticules ("ridicules") since the pocket would have revealed its outline under the slim skirts of the Regency. The early reticules were similar in shape to the previously concealed pockets (Fig. 2–21). In her reticule, a woman might carry a miniature of her sweetheart, a writing tablet, letters, and paper packets of rouge or other cosmetics. Framed purses, with a hooked catch or a press-button opening, became more popular toward 1820. Reticules were made to be decorative items in themselves, often

Fig. 2–22

matching the fabric of the gown. Some reticules were made of knitted silk with steel or glass beading. French beading techniques mimicked purses made of flowers, and other light themes. Solid bead fabrics were used for bags from Germany.

Scarlet cloaks (think of Little Red Riding Hood) were popular in 1800, but lost favor by 1830 (Fig. 2–22).

Men wore breeches early in the Regency, then pantalons as skin-tight as the breeches had become, extending to the ankles but worn under boots. Simple, undecorated fabrics were the rule, though some selected a fine, striped material. The most popular fabric for pantalons was wool, because it stretched well to fit snugly. It should be pointed out that the tight pants needed to be gathered in the back, so the man could sit down. (Think in terms of a cloth diaper!) Some dandies remained standing rather than wear such an unattractive cut. Of course, the coat usually covered the back of the pants anyway, which did wonders for the aesthetics of fashion. Later years produced pantaloons, which were cut fuller in the front and worn with slippers. All types of pants were usually in a white or light tan fabric, as were the stockings or socks.

A shirt was considered part of the "undress." It was worn with a single-breasted waistcoat over it, then a frock coat or tail coat over that. Men wore a starched neckcloth or cravat at the neck. If not folded and pleated correctly, the starching would result in creases, which is why a man might go through several neckcloths before getting one folded and pleated to his satisfaction. A heavily starched neckcloth of linen was uncomfortable. (And a linen neckcloth plus woolen pants is a combination that sounds itchy all over.)

Boots such as Hessians were replaced by short boots, and then by low-heeled slippers as the years progressed. A heel was necessary on men's shoes, to anchor the trouser strap of pantaloons. Boots sometimes had built-in decorative spurs, and were popular for walking in 1817–19. (The spurs were worn to be fashionable — not for riding unruly horses.)

A man might wear stays (as in a corset), laced in the back, to make his waistline smaller. He might also pad his coat a bit, though this was more popular in the Victorian era.

Tricorns of the eighteenth century were replaced by tall crowned hats with curled brims. A man might accessorize with short gloves, watches, fobs, walking canes and, of course, a quizzing glass.

VICTORIAN ERA

The Victorian Era saw some of the most widespread changes in women's fashions to date. Layers of petticoats led to more practical bustles and hoopskirts. These reached extraordinary size and then went completely out of style during the 1880s. After the ex-

Turn-of-the-century two-piece black suit. This elaborately beaded costume is worn here by Elan MacIntosh. Suit from the collection of Barbara Temperley; used by permission.

tremely tapered skirts of the 1880s, full skirts returned but in more sensible proportions, which led the way for a more natural, flattering series of fashions for women.

In addition to skirt widths, other aspects of fashion changed rapidly through the nineteenth century. High-necked gowns with numerous collars led to a dropped shoulderline and then a wide neck opening that eventually was off-the-shoulder. Ballooning oversleeves led to flared oversleeves and, finally, to simple, single sleeves, such as short puffed sleeves. The somber colors of the early Victorian years led to colors that reflected the time of year when the garment would be worn. These were then replaced by bright, intense colors made possible by aniline dyes. Yet women over 40 began wearing black for all occasions. In the latter Victorian years, the pastels of the eighteenth century were briefly back in fashion, before darker colors returned to style.

As you can see, if you're representing the Victorian era, it is difficult to generalize about the clothing, and I recommend that you use the references listed in this book, plus whatever is available at your public library. Fortunately, you can study photographs and illustrated magazines from the Victorian era, which are some of the best references available.

AMERICAN CIVIL WAR EPOCH

While certainly a part of the Victorian era, the Civil War years are one of the most popular periods among individuals interested in costuming and reproduction clothing, and thus deserve a separate discussion.

American women selected their fabrics from a wide variety available, including cotton, wool, silk, velvet, satin, poplin, taffeta, and alpaca. Aniline dyes had just appeared, so women selected brilliant and intense colors. Browns and blacks remained, especially on women over age 40, but there were also rich purples, blues, and bottle greens.

Trims were often ornate applications of flat braid and decorative ribbons. More than one type of decoration was often used.

The basic item in all women's clothing was the hoopskirt, also called a crinoline, although it was no longer the horsehair

Fig. 2–23

Fig. 2–24

crinoline of early Victorian years. The hoopskirt was a series of metal rings (or, occasionally, whalebone) held together by a slip-like garment or a series of strips of fabric (Fig. 2–23). The hoop did not simply make the skirt look full, it also supported the heavy weight of the skirt. On a hot summer day, I'm certain that many ladies appreciated the comfort of the hoop instead of being wrapped in the dozen petticoats that preceeded it in fashion.

Petticoats were still worn, *over* the hoopskirt, to give a softer look and to conceal the ridges of the hoops.

A corset was laced to constrict the waist and make the bustline look rounder by comparison. By the way, it is important to note that corset edges rarely met when laced. An 18″ corset did not necessarily mean an 18″ waist when the woman was laced into it. She might have a 20″ or 22″ waist when laced, because the sides of the corset were several inches apart when correctly worn. So, if you buy a corset for the perfect Civil War impression, you should follow the size guidelines of the person selling the corset. A corset in your exact waist size will be too big to lace correctly. Needless to say, many women laced their corsets as tightly as they could. During this era, smelling salts were a necessity to revive fainting women whose lungs were restricted by the tight corset. The stories about ribs being broken or surgically removed are not true. Fashionable women may have been vain, but they certainly weren't mad.

Undergarments, including stockings, were sometimes bright red in this era. White was preferred, but red was a novelty and petticoats and drawers were often made of red flannel or cashmere.

Most gowns of the time had a dropped shoulder to make a woman look as if she had extremely sloped shoulders (Fig. 2–24). Seams were placed to enhance this appearance, and to make the back look narrow. Daytime dresses usually fastened in the front with buttons, hooks and eyes, or some sort of lacing. Ball gowns and evening wear usually fastened in back, with some sort of lacing preferred for a smooth, delicate appearance.

Women had to move with gliding steps; hasty or or careless movements caused a hoopskirt to bob or swing. If you've watched *Gone with the Wind* closely, you've seen underwear revealed by a running woman. When sitting, the back of the crinoline was lifted slightly, so that the hoopskirt collapsed a bit. The alternative was to have it bell up around the chin.

Speaking of underwear in movies, the long *pantalettes* in many early movies depicting the Civil War are incorrect. Those were from an earlier era. Drawers in the Civil War years reached the knee or mid-calf at the longest.

A fire hazard was also posed by an uncontrolled hoopskirt. In an era of large fireplaces and candlelight, it was easy to topple a lamp or swing one's skirt too near the fire. And, furthermore, the skirt made it impossible to roll on the floor to put out the fire, as we're instructed today. I've read about a hoopskirt filled with water in the hoop area, so that a woman could fall to the floor if her gown caught fire, and the water would burst through the skirt and douse the fire. This is likely just a rumor; water would have been very heavy to carry in a skirt.

The water-filled hoopskirt is an example of one of the most ridiculous ideas of this era. We don't know if it was actually worn by women, and in planning historical clothing, you need to think in practical terms. Use common sense. Of course, you should read the magazines and books of the time, to see what they illustrate. *Godey's* was the most popular Civil-War-era women's magazine, and you can get color copies of its fashion illustrations from Heidi Marsh (see Resources listing). However, don't follow them blindly. For example, *Godey's* shoes seem to be uniformly square-toed. I wear a round-toed, laced-up boot that is not only the most comfortable footwear I own, but is "correct" for the time, as well. Just as you aren't likely to wear something out of the pages of *Vogue* when you go to work or do your grocery shopping, Civil War ladies did not spend all of their time wearing fashions from *Godey's* pages.

Men were emerging from the narrow-waisted, sloped-shoulder look. The frock coat was still popular, but the shoulders were now square-cut. Men's chests looked broader with the coats' new, lower waistlines. A waistcoat (a sort of vest, usually with its own collar) was also worn, frequently matching the fabric of the trousers. A waistcoat might also have been made of wonderful, rich colors or even a heavily embroidered brocade. A sack suit was fashionable, but only for less formal occasions.

Men's trousers were loose, with no creases at front and back. The fly front was popular, but zippers had not been invented and buttons were used. Some men decorated the side seams of their trousers with braid.

Men wore suspenders, called "braces." They did have elastic in those days, although it was different from what we use today and elastic was not used in braces at that time. The braces ranged from plain to incredibly ornate with needlework decorations.

Men had full wardrobes. That is, to be fully dressed, a gentleman wore many items and carried several accessories. It was a time of stiff, formal movement, with a strong, self-conscious sense of dignity.

For a complete description of Civil War clothing, many resources are available. Some of my favorites are listed in the References section, but I most heartily recommend *Clothing Guidelines for the Civil War Era* by Janet Burgess. If you supplement this book with any of the well-illustrated *Civil War Ladies Sketchbooks* by K. A. York, you'll be able to plan your wardrobe easily. Authentic illustrations from the hoop era are available from Heidi Marsh, in black-and-white and in color. These illustrations will give you costuming ideas to make your clothing look both correct and spectacular.

THE GAY NINETIES

The 1890s ushered in a series of delightful, flattering years of women's fashions. After some extreme and restrictive fashions, particularly in the early 1880s, clothing was now softer and more practical. Life was more fun. Henry James, H. G. Wells, Oscar Wilde, Rudyard Kipling, and George Bernard Shaw were among the popular writers of the time. Music was by Strauss, Borodin, Tchaikovsky, and Mahler. The Olympic Games were being organized. The safety razor was invented. Iron and steel workers went on strike in the U.S. Utah became a state. Grover Cleveland and William McKinley were presidents during the 1890s. Victoria had celebrated her Golden Jubilee, and still reigned as Queen of England. Marconi invented radio telegraphy, Freud was writing his papers, and Benz and Ford were building cars. Eastman perfected the Kodak box camera. Dunlop invented pneumatic tires. Edison's electrical lamps were lighting homes. It was a progressive, exciting era.

Fig. 2–25

Women's clothing was basically simple. Skirts were flat in front and fuller to the sides and back. The shoulders were broad and sleeves were full, especially at the shoulder line. It should be mentioned that the sleeves puffed *out*, not *up*. They are often referred to as "leg o'mutton" sleeves, and various forms of padding or structured support were used to maintain the shape of the larger sleeves. Blouses (waists) were often fashioned after men's clothes for daily wear, with high, starched collars. Women wore waistcoats that matched their skirts and jackets, for the look of a three-piece suit. Colors were intense, and didn't necessarily go together well. One of the favorite colors was yellow. Fashionable women still laced their waistlines in tight corsets, but hoopskirts were no longer in style. Skirts were cut to allow a wide stride when walking. Hats were diverse, ranging from small to huge, and all perched on top of the hair and were held in place with pins. Hair styles were severe and simple at the back, with small curls at the forehead. It was the era of the Gibson Girl. Veils were in fashion, as were large, heavily decorated collars. Styles became flamboyant and reflected personal tastes. Part of this was due to the invention of the sewing machine, which reduced the time and expense necessary to create a garment. In the 1890s, it became easier to follow the brief extremes of fashion.

Men's fashions continued along their former lines. Sack suits were seen more frequently. Frock coats were longer, with shorter waists (Fig. 2–25). Fabrics were generally softer, though shirt collars remained high and well-starched. There was a certain flair to the way men's clothing flowed, which softened their mannered demeanor. Patent leather shoes with pointed toes were worn in the evening. Casual day wear might include white flannel trousers and dark jackets, particularly in the summer. Men still carried many accessories, including a walking cane, card case, gloves, and cigarette case. Think in terms of the PBS Mystery series, *Sherlock Holmes*. Understated style, refinement, and unsurpassed elegance.

Fig. 2–26

EDWARDIAN ERA

King Edward VII ruled from 1901 to 1910, and many consider Edwardian fashions to rival the Regency for elegance and romance.

Fig. 2–27

Fig. 2–28

Women wore soft, feminine fabrics with lots of lace (Figs. 2–26 and 2–27). Fashionable fabrics included chiffon, muslin, lawn, mohair, and clingy velvets. Colors were carefully planned for a harmonious appearance. The hourglass figure was idolized, and women padded bust and hips to achieve the desired appearance. Gowns fit snugly around the hips, and flared out to swirl around the lower legs when the woman moved (Fig. 2–28). In addition to laces, fabric decorations included bead embroidery, frills, braiding, spangles, lace inserts, fabric flowers, feathers, and ribbons. Tea dresses from this era are particularly popular among collectors, but difficult to find in wearable condition since the original fabrics were so delicate.

Men's fashions were simpler and bolder in design, but basically the same as in preceeding years. Plaids were out of fashion, and the only stylish patterned fabric was a simple stripe, such as pin striping. Men continued to carry themselves "correctly," though artifice was beginning to come under scrutiny.

A good guideline to the late Victorian and Edwardian periods is the Masterpiece Theatre series, *Upstairs, Downstairs.*

TWENTIETH CENTURY IN BRIEF

Hemlines began to climb after the Edwardian period, new dyes and fibers were created, and former fashion restrictions were relaxed, all allowing more frequent changes in style from year to year.

Larger public libraries have books and magazines from the early twentieth century which will give you these fashions in detail. The general costume books recommended in the References section are also good guidelines for the diverse styles of this century. You can easily research these years in depth yourself.

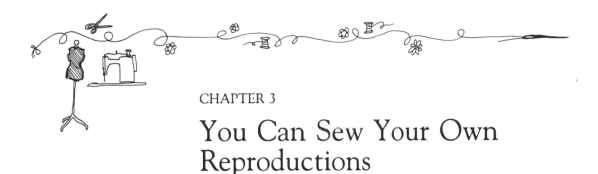

CHAPTER 3

You Can Sew Your Own Reproductions

Really! No matter what your level of sewing skill, you can sew your own costumes. Even if you think costuming is too difficult, read this chapter: You'll find some items will be easy enough to tackle, and that may lead you to bigger and better things. Chapter 4 tells you the easy, no-frills way to sew a quick costume. Whether you're sewing an authentic masterpiece or a hasty party costume, you'll need the information in this chapter about selecting materials.

First, you must decide how accurate you want your costume to be, and how to define *accurate*. The two schools of thought on this are:

1. The strict definition of accuracy, used by people who believe that everything should be clearly documentable. With book plates, magazines, paintings, and other art of the time, plus actual garments, tradesmen's swatches, and household inventories, we can find actual examples of enough garments to have an entire, accurate outfit for historical purposes. In this school of thought, there is no reason to speculate, because there are many documented styles of clothing and it is important to show only what actually existed.

"Merilee" is typical of Civil War era gowns with embroidered braces. Designed and modeled by Harriet Engler, costume consultant for the North & South miniseries. Photo courtesy of Harriet A. Engler, Tailoring-Custom Sewing.

Fig. 3-1

2. A more flexible definition of accuracy is shared by people who believe that many more styles existed than are shown in paintings, books, and so on. A woman might have compensated for limited materials or sewing skills by changing a popular design. She may have been influenced by clothing from her childhood, by a traveler from another area, or by her own whimsy. Perhaps a wealthy relative gave her an outdated ballgown, and she altered the gown and wore it to milk the cows. The possibilities are endless. This group includes people who are making costumes for non-historical purposes. It includes people who are simply bored with the same old gowns that they've seen in paintings, and are being as creative as their historical counterparts may have been. The limits are less clearly defined, and this is where the purists get concerned. We do not want to give the public an inaccurate idea of historical dressing. It's jarring to see a Colonial farmer wearing breeches with belt loops and a zipper fly. A Medieval woman would not have machine-sewn topstitching on her gown. And I wince when I see a Regency gown made from synthetic knit fabrics. Creativity is great, but inaccuracy is not.

I belong to the second group. If it could have existed, I wear it to show the diversity of the time. However, living history interpreters are often challenged on their facts, and it is important to be able to document claims with real evidence. I recommend that you stay within historically proven bounds until you've done enough research to know what could have existed, and what was impossible for a given era.

PATTERNS

If you have little or no sewing skill, you'll want easy patterns. Even if you've never made clothing before, you can still use simple patterns with great results.

Use common sense. If you are horrid at tailoring, avoid jackets and coats. If you hate cutting out a zillion pieces, check the envelope before you select your pattern. Some of the larger historical pattern companies illustrate the number of pieces on the back of the pattern envelope. Others do not, and you'll need to actually look in the envelope to see how many pieces are required in the garment of your choice.

Fig. 3-2

What if you're in love with a pattern that is entirely beyond your expertise? You'll have to be creative in your approach. Get someone else to cut it out, if you don't have the patience. Or cut the pattern pieces yourself, and then have a seamstress do the major construction work. Or you might sew until you are fed up with the job, and then turn the remainder over to a seamstress. If none of these alternatives appeal, you might hand the pattern and materials to a seamstress and have her do the whole thing.

You can find a variety of commercial patterns for any time period. Some are more accurate than others. Some are deliberately simple; you can make an adequate gown for costume wear, or adapt it to match an image you've seen.

One example of simple, adaptable patterns is the line by Pegee of Williamsburg. For her eras, I cannot imagine simpler patterns. They're ideal for beginners, and for those of us who want to add extra, fun details to really personalize our clothing. Her Colonial gown took me less than a day to make and I barely had to look at the instructions.

However, while simple patterns are adequate for my use, I have had purists criticize my enthusiastic endorsement of them. Frankly, I would have made simple gowns in historical days. Between tending the garden, taking care of the children, and running my husband's business while he was off at war, I wouldn't have had time to sew anything more detailed. I recognize that certain additions and changes may be desired by someone who wants a gown that is exactly like something they've seen in a painting or a history book. But that's a matter of interpretation. You'll have to decide for yourself. And check with the group you're appearing with, to see what its standards are.

If you're new to historical clothing, I recommend looking over the full range of patterns from a company such as Amazon Dry Goods. You'll get a nice overview and save a *lot* of money in the process, since you're only writing to one shop. Once you've decided what kind of pattern you'd like, you can always write to the business owner (in the case of Amazon, that is Janet Burgess) and ask her about a particular design you'd like.

Each company's own catalogue may illustrate more of their patterns. But in most cases you can still buy the same patterns

You Can Sew Your Own Reproductions

from a general company, such as Amazon, which saves handling fees, if you're ordering patterns by several manufacturers.

If you are an unusual size, you may find it surprisingly easy to locate your size among historical patterns. Contemporary pattern companies need to keep up with changing fashions and print patterns only in the most popular sizes. Historical pattern companies have no similar pressure. They can enhance their lines by adding unusual sizes; their styles will remain popular indefinitely.

Bellow Canto in Victorian performance, 1987. The L.A.-based musical group provides period vocals to accompany historic events. Photo courtesy of Jenny Reily.

SEWING AND COLLECTING VINTAGE FASHIONS

Some pattern designers will create custom sizes and styles for you. One such designer is Heidi Marsh, who specializes in "The Era of the Hoop," which includes the Civil War years. (See Resources list for address.) It takes one to five full eight-hour days for Mrs. Marsh to complete an entirely new pattern. She has made custom-sized patterns for men to a 64″ chest, and women to a 56″ bust.

Mail-order is not the only source of historical patterns. Check with local pattern dealers. In historic areas, such as Concord, Massachusetts, I've found historical patterns to be part of the regular stock at fabric shops. If you're in a hurry, Folkwear patterns are carried in most major fabric stores. (At press time, Folkwear is undergoing management changes which may affect the availability of these wonderful patterns.) Some of their patterns are ideal for a particular era, while their ethnic patterns can be adapted for historical use in a pinch. After all, many are designs that have been used for centuries.

No matter which is your favorite era, certain styles are similar to present-day patterns. Many contemporary wedding gown and formalwear patterns are perfectly at home in Victorian and Edwardian settings. Laura Ashley and Ralph Lauren feature patterns and readymades that are drawn from the past 150 years. And when I used an old 1930s pattern (which I found at a yard sale) to make a skirt for a murder mystery party, I was dismayed to discover the same design in two contemporary pattern lines. (And both their instructions and fit would have been superior to the old pattern that I used.)

Of course, when you use an authentic pattern from a reputable company, you can be certain of the styling and fit of the finished garment. In general, I do not recommend buying old patterns at yard sales, unless you are experienced in altering patterns to fit your body shape. In fact, it appears that the Civil War years are the most popular in many companies, since there are more patterns available for this era than any other.

Saundra Ros Altman, owner of Past Patterns, confirmed that her most popular patterns are from the 1860s. However, she has also noticed that customers' interests are reinforced by the fashion market and such magazines as *Vogue* and *Sew News*. During one year, 1920s may be popular, the next year more customers may want 1930s patterns.

Victorian Shawl....

made into a bustle

Fig. 3–3

No matter what your era, if you are sewing your own gown, you should think about sewing the other parts of your wardrobe as well. Do not overlook undergarments. Corsets varied widely from era to era, so select one that matches your time period exactly. Several pattern companies in the Resources listing carry corset patterns and kits. You can also buy a readymade corset, but be certain that it's for "your" year. Past Patterns carries several corset options, which will make a tremendous difference in the appearance of your costume. And you'll fall in love with the rest of their patterns, too. Order your size according to the company's recommendations; corset size is rarely the same as your actual waistline measurement.

Likewise, you'll want to look into hoopskirts and bustles. They're vital to appearance and comfort during certain eras. In many cases, you can buy readymades for so little that it is hardly worth sewing them. I have an antique bustle that I wear with some Victorian clothes. It was made so that the hip dimensions adjust by pulling cords inside the bustle, and I can wear it with nearly all Victorian fashions. For other eras, I have a reproduction hoopskirt. Over both, I wear early-twentieth-century petticoats, which were more affordable than sewing reproduction petticoats. I also have *real* old drawers that I wear for warmth (those metal hoops are *cold*) in the winter.

Needless to say, you should never wear antique clothing of historic significance. For example, I own a ladies' fan from the Wolcott family, related to one of the signers of the Declaration of Independence. It remains under glass, displayed in my collection. By contrast, I bought a shredded silk Victorian cape at an auction. Its original owner was unknown and the garment was too damaged to be suitable for display. I stitched and fused the cape to stronger fabric, and then gathered it to make an attractive bustle (Fig. 3–3). It is now a vital part of my Victorian wardrobe.

If you discover clothing that is unusually old and in perfect condition, or an item that belonged to someone of importance, save it for your non-wearable collection, or donate it to a museum or living history site.

Camisoles are another necessity if you're in the Victorian era (Fig. 3–4). Before you take the time to sew one, check stores that carry imported clothing from India and Mexico. I made a wonderful silk-satin camisole from a design by Past Patterns and I love it.

Fig. 3-4

But for everyday wear, I choose the Mexican camisole that cost me a few dollars and can be thrown into the washing machine without hesitation.

Hats are easier to make than you might expect. Several companies offer patterns and materials for making old-fashioned hats and bonnets. One company, The Wonderful World of Hats (see Resources) offers a complete correspondence course on making historical hats. Because hats were exposed to the elements, and made of fragile materials in the first place, reproduction hats are often your only choice.

FABRICS

Let me tell you the bad news first: You probably don't want to buy synthetic fabrics, or even synthetic blends. Yes, I know they're affordable, they look great in the store, and who wants to iron a 13-yard skirt of badly wrinkled cotton!

The fact is, if you're making a costume for one-time wear at a party, a synthetic might be okay. But think about this: Synthetic fabrics do not breathe as well as natural fibers. If the weather is hot, or you're in a crowd, you'll feel as if you're in a steam bath. Especially in a long skirt or gown.

Fig. 3-5

If the weather is cold, you'll find it harder to get warm and comfortable in synthetic fabrics. Synthetics just don't have that cozy feeling. And once you do start feeling warm, it's usually because the steam-bath effect has started. Soon you'll be perspiring underneath your garment, and will positively freeze when you go back outside in the cold weather.

Then there is appearance. Synthetics don't seem to take dyes the same as natural fibers do. They may look fine in the store, but you'll see the difference when you're next to a gown of natural fibers. You can probably get away with a synthetic cummerbund, but all those yards and yards in a gown will certainly reveal the basically plastic nature of the fabric. And even if the colors are fine (which is rare), you'll discover that synthetics have a sheen that natural fibers never get. Except for knits. I don't find that synthetics drape as flatteringly as natural fibers, either. (And knits certainly aren't accurate.)

I once made a wonderful Colonial skirt in a synthetic blend. It had just a little polyester in it, I rationalized. Besides, it was so affordable. It took me a full day to arrange the gathers so that I was happy with it. Then another day of hand sewing, for authenticity. The rest of my costume was entirely natural fibers, including the overskirt. It looked spectacular when I was in full costume.

Fig. 3–6

The outfit looked great at the amateur parades and events. And at 5:30 a.m. on Lexington Green, who was awake enough to discern snythetic from natural? When the baby spilled his bottle on my gown, it was a quick wash-and-dry, and I was ready to wear it again. At the time, I was thrilled with my skirt. However, I quickly changed my mind.

It was a gorgeous day for a parade in Wilmington, Massachusetts. My family and I were in our Colonial garb, and the skies were clear. The parade started, we marched with our unit, and the sun got hotter. Before long, I discovered that I was perspiring heavily beneath my skirt, while I was comfortably cool from the waist up. My all-cotton petticoat was soaking up the perspiration, getting heavier and heavier, while my skirt kept the heat in. I finally said, "Oh, to heck with it," and raised my skirt to let in the fresh air. It was such a relief. And every few minutes for the rest of the afternoon, I was doing my best to discreetly let the air circulate.

My next disappointment with the skirt was a few weeks later in Lexington. Every two years, Revolutionary groups get together to re-enact the battles along Battle Road, which includes Concord and Lexington. Some of the best costumes are seen there. Next to those wonderful, authentic costumes by women who'd used the correct fabrics, my grey skirt looked so bright and shiny that it stood out like a neon sign. Needless to say, we didn't stay at the battles for long.

Since then, I've been warned that synthetic fabrics catch fire before cottons do. (If you have any doubt about that, check the heat settings on your iron.) Since many living history events take place with open fires, candles, and/or fireplaces, it is smarter to wear cotton, linen, or wool.

There is one final reason to avoid synthetics. In time, many will get little balls of thread on them, often called "pills." Sure, natural fibers get them too, but you can pull them off the natural fibers. Synthetic fibers are so much stronger that, when you pull off one pill, it will bring with it enough thread to start another one. It becomes a never-ending chore, once the pilling starts.

If you're going to put the time into making an authentic garment (especially if you do the sewing by hand), get an authentic fabric.

Do natural fibers mean endless ironing? Well, if you pre-shrink your fabrics so that they are machine washable and dryable, you can take your gown out of the dryer promptly and hang it right up. Most wrinkles won't have a chance to form. And if you're a complete perfectionist, you can take your clothes to your nearby laundry or dry cleaner, and ask them to do the pressing for you. It is well worth dealing with the wrinkles to use a natural fiber.

And when wearing your natural fiber clothing in a situation where it might get stained, you should consider protecting with Scotchgard or a similar stain-repellant. Of course, if clothing does get stained, you can always point out that it's more authentic that way.

Preshrink fabrics before you sew them, if you're planning to wash the garments after you wear them. The dryer heat-shrinks fabrics more than washing does. I usually put my laundered fabric through the dryer with my regular laundry loads, until it has had at least 3 hours of dryer heat. This ensures that the fabric won't shrink in repeated launderings. If you forget to preshrink your fabrics, you should wash them on a gentle cycle the first few times, and line dry them. For some reason, after this there is less shrinkage when you finally try them in dryer heat.

The good news is that several companies carry some excellent, unusual, authentic fabrics. Amazon Dry Goods carries fabrics and some notions for nineteenth-century clothing and accessories. Many regular sewing shops, plus some mail-order sources listed in Resources in the back of this book, carry handwoven fabrics that are suitable for many eras. If you have an unlimited budget and want something unique, you can probably have a local weaver custom-weave fabric to your specifications.

If you're planning a delicate tea gown, you'll find today's natural fibers are ideal, and their scope is tremendous. However, before you buy a dozen yards of silk satin, get a quarter yard and try sewing a few seams. See if you can find straight pins (also called common pins in certain parts of the country) that won't leave

holes in the fabric (see listing for Clotilde in Resources). Find out how long you can use your sewing machine needle before it snags the silk. And test your patience with the constant slipping of the fabric.

There are tricks to sewing on slippery fabrics, which you'll learn from friends who sew, or from sewing books at the public library. Among the best are: use a walking foot on your sewing machine, so that the upper and lower layers of fabric move through the machine together; use a fine thread that matches the fiber on which you're sewing, so that it doesn't snag or drag the fabric; se-

lect the best possible needle for your machine (some are made for fine sewing on slippery fabrics) and change it as soon as it becomes dull. I know few people who are willing to sew on silk satin. There are alternatives which are not so soft or shiny, but will give a pleasing effect nevertheless. A rough-textured silk will be easier to handle and will lend a charming, glistening sheen to your garment. A sheer cotton with an interesting weave will stain less and be more practical than most silks. The bridal section of the fabric store may have other alternatives. Choose one of these fabrics, and you'll still have your sense of humor when you complete the garment.

For Victorian brocades, be certain to shop at stores featuring upholstery fabrics. Their heavy cottons can be tremendous, too. If you're recreating fashions from an era when Paisley was popular, some of my favorite Paisley fabrics were intended for interior decor. Heavy upholstery braid can be the Victorian trim you need, as well.

NOTIONS

For the usual reason of authenticity, it is wise to get buttons or other fastenings that are correct. That isn't as difficult as it sounds. Most sewing shops carry buttons in wood and other natural materials. Jet buttons, popular during the Victorian era, are still available. And most antique and second-hand shops can help you with some affordable "real" buttons if you shop around a bit. If you're considering real mother-of-pearl buttons, remember that they chip easily and can separate into layers during repeated washing. I use them anyway, because they look so much better than the plastic alternatives.

You can conceal (thoroughly, please) zippers, Velcro, and other modern closures, if you want a contemporary fit in a garment that could not otherwise conform to your figure. For reasons of decency, I've had to conceal some closures in my Colonial gown bodice because I haven't taken the time to add the dozen extra hooks that will keep the panel closed. Frankly, contemporary closures, even when fully concealed, detract from the accuracy of the final appearance. If you're using a pattern that fits you, and you're using historically accurate closures, but you still want to conceal some Velcro. . .well, just realize that the original garment couldn't have fit that well. As long as it isn't indecent, perhaps you'll become accustomed to the fit. And you can also check with others, to see how they got *their* clothing to fit.

Don't buy real old thread. I've bought hundreds of spools at auctions and yard sales. Their 100 percent cotton content delighted me — until I used them. I don't know if it was the age of the thread, or whether I'm spoiled by today's blended threads, but I found that the old thread broke too frequently to use. I still buy old spools of thread, but that's because I'm planning a display of the old wooden spools and threads. And I love to have old sewing materials in my sewing room.

I prefer to buy the most expensive, imported brands of thread. They seem to break less often, and are of more uniform thickness than other brands. Of course, this may have something to do with the kind of electric sewing machine I have. If your machine was not designed for lightweight, Styrofoam spools, you may be happier with the imported threads. Some come on heavy plastic spools which don't bounce around during a flurry of sewing. If you're going to use pure cotton thread, check that it has been pre-shrunk before you use it, or it will pucker your fabric on its first visit to the washing machine. I know some women who place the thread, spool and all, in a pot of boiling water to preshrink it. I've never tried this because I usually use blended cotton thread, and it does not shrink. (See Resources mail-order sources of thread.)

When you do your shopping, buy extra of everything. If you tend to change dress sizes often, it's wise to buy some extra fabric. Whether you're adding inches to a costume during early pregnancy, or replacing an entire gown section that was stained (or got caught in the car door), extra fabric can be a blessing. Historical costuming is usually worn for more years than your average garment, so size changes and stains are more likely. Take a tip from clothing manufacturers, and sew a few extra buttons somewhere inside the garment. If you lose one of the twenty buttons that closes the back of your bodice, it's great to be able to replace it easily. If the buttons are no longer made, replacing the other nineteen could be a nightmare.

SELECTING COLORS

First of all, learn what "your" colors are. Yes, yes, I know that this sounds too trendy to take seriously, but look at it this way: If you're going to buy a $10 pattern, 10 yards of fabric, and then spend a couple of weeks sewing it, the finished gown had better look terrific on you. A color may be fine in a contemporary skirt far away from your face, but you can't hide from the color when it covers you from chin to toe. Besides, you're probably going to wear this gown for several years to make your investment worthwhile. If you aren't certain that the color was right in the first place, you'll never be entirely happy with your gown. And that can spoil the fun of the events that you made the gown for in the first place.

I had my colors analyzed, free of charge, by one of the many BeautiControl consultants. Sure, I had read the books on choosing which "season" reflected my best colors, but I was only 90 percent certain that I'd chosen my season correctly. Ten minutes with the woman from BeautiControl showed me, very clearly, that I was wrong in my original choice. A few months later, I spent a couple of hours with Mary Kay consultant Claire Molloy, who showed me even more about color, and helped me see which prints would work best in my clothing. If you don't know your colors (or aren't quite certain), these addresses are in the Resources listing at the back of the book. Don't put time and money into a garment if you aren't certain that the results will be spectacular.

For women, there is an added benefit to having your colors analyzed: I don't know how you look without makeup, but I look *much* better with a little added color here and there. I'm one of those people with porcelain-pale skin, and I always feel as if I'm fading into the woodwork when I don't add a bit of oomph. However, there is nothing that looks so out-of-place (if not downright cheap) as visible makeup in a historical re-enactment. So my consultants helped me choose colors that blended right in with my natural/historical look, cannot be detected (even by my mother!), but make me feel more attractive than I would if I didn't wear makeup. With a bit of color, I can feel confident next to those makeup-less beauties who were born with pink cheeks and have naturally dark, long eyelashes. If you use mascara, use a light touch; and remember that colored eyeshadow is going to look ridiculous.

Speaking of makeup, nail polish is generally inappropriate prior to the twentieth century. If you have weak nails that need constant protection, get the false nails that look natural in color.

My skin tends to look blotchy when I'm cold or when I'm out in the sun for a while. It took me years to find a foundation that doesn't turn color or look chalky after a few hours (the brand is Mary Kay, which amazed me, because I thought all foundations were pretty similar). So I do wear well-blended foundation at im-

Fig. 3–7

portant events. But I recommend that you wear only as much makeup as looks perfectly natural. And if you know which colors look like Mother Nature put them there, you can enhance your appearance if necessary. Remember that most of the young women at the event will not be wearing makeup. If you use as much makeup as you wear to work, you'll look "painted."

Once you know which families of colors look best on you, you'll need to know which of those colors are historically accurate for your time period. If your library has a good needlework section, you should be able to find a book showing the actual colors obtained when using natural dyes. Books such as *Fabric of Society* by Jane Tozier, a Laura Ashley book, show photos of actual fabrics of the eras they cover. And many needlework stores will have color cards from yarn companies showing naturally dyed fibers. These are your best references, combined with history books that describe textiles.

Remember to check your time period for the *number of colors* in the average outfit. During some eras, monochromatic colors were "in," while other periods excelled in combining a variety of colors for different effects. Another factor in choosing colors: If you're planning to put braid on your skirt, select a fabric that matches the braid that you want.

For your first complex garment, I'd recommend a solid color. If you use a fabric with nap, or one with a design that has to be positioned "just so," with all the flowers or figures right-side-up and matched at the seams, you may find yourself abandoning the project before it's completed. If you absolutely must have a fabric with a design, I recommend fabrics intended for quilting that are always "upside up," no matter which way you hold the fabric. My favorite is "Jinny Beyer dots" in midnight blue. (I'm not certain what it's really called; this is the name we quilters use.) Also, you'll find some extraordinary designs from Jeff Gutcheon. For Victorian wear, some of his hauntingly dark combinations are marvelous. These are most often found in shops that specialize in cottons for quilters, but they can be purchased by mail as well. See the Resources section in the back of the book for these fabrics.

CONSTRUCTING A GARMENT

Cutting Out Pattern Pieces

Cutting out all the pieces can be the most difficult part, and the most important. Particularly in the Victorian years, certain body types were popular and the cut of clothing was planned to emphasize particular features. For example, sloped shoulders were admired in the first half of the nineteenth century. Shoulder seams were planned to keep the shoulder line as smooth as possible, and to make the back look narrow. However, when cutting pattern pieces for the bodice, you must plan so that you'll have enough "give" in the back to move! Your pattern instructions will guide you, and it is important to follow them exactly.

In my experience, it is easier to construct a Victorian gown than it is to lay out and cut all the fabric pieces, but don't be overwhelmed. It isn't hard; it just requires care and patience. If someone else is going to do all the sewing for you, you might consider the economy of cutting out the pattern yourself. Why pay a seamstress to do a job that you can do? Of course, if you are planning to sew your gown at the end of an 8-hour workday, pay someone to do the cutting for you. Then you can handle the easier job of sewing the garment.

Fig. 3–8

Lay out all the pieces before you start cutting. Check the envelope an extra time. Look around the floor in case you forgot a piece or two. I can usually find a more economical way to lay out my pattern pieces without changing their position relative to the grain. However, it's easy to forget a piece when you have twenty or thirty of them.

Hand versus Machine Sewing

Sewing machines were not popular until the end of the nineteenth century. If you are creating a Medieval, Colonial or Regency garment, do not use the sewing machine in places where the stitches will show. Most Victorian clothing should not show machine stitching, either.

Now, you're going to laugh at this, but I'm going to make a plea for handsewing. Yes, it can take forever, but you can sew in front of the TV or when talking on the phone, and it really can be a pleasure. If you sew with a double thread and backstitch every fourth stitch, you'll have a really well-made garment. And the fabric will drape more softly than if you used a sewing machine. You will love the look. And you'll feel marvelously superior when you wear the clothes, because you'll know that they are entirely accurate.

Fig. 3–9

My favorite sewing machine, for any purpose, is my Standard treadle machine. I pump it with my feet, the wheels spin around, and the needle goes evenly up and down. In fact, it runs so evenly that I can back up the needle in the holes it just sewed, if I need to rip out a section. It pulls the thread right back out. In addition, the stitches are more even than those produced by my expensive electric machine. The only sewing machine that can rival my treadle is a professional-quality sewing machine. And I buy my treadle machines (I own several) for less than $25 each. They are simple enough to oil and repair myself. The thread rarely breaks, and my tension is always correct. There is something comforting in the rhythm of the treadle at the end of an exhausting day.

If you are planning to follow my advice and buy a treadle, here are some tips: First of all, don't pay more than $50 for one, even with the world's most gorgeous cabinet. My Standard cost me $15, including all attachments, instruction booklet and the oak cabinet. They will sell for different prices in different areas, depending on popular demand, but show the owner this book if the price tag says more than $50. If the leather belt is worn or missing, you can replace that easily through a good sewing machine repair service. Turn the wheel at the end of the machine to move the needle up and down. If it doesn't budge, take a look at what's underneath the machine. I carry some WD-40 and paper towels with me, to clean and oil dirty, dry, or rusted machines. If the needle seems "frozen" after I use WD-40, I leave the machine. Or I buy it for $5 if it is exactly like another machine I own, so that I'll have spare parts. Spare parts are rarely necessary; I've never had to replace more than a missing footplate.

Check the bobbin on your treadle machine. Some models, particularly New Home machines, have a shuttle-style bobbin. I have never used one of these, but a friend of mine swears by her New Home treadle. Some models have *no* bobbin, because they are chain-stitch machines and all the thread comes from the spool. I have one of these, simply because the machine looks so nice. I rarely use it because the stitches rip out easily if the thread is not well-secured at the start and end of each seam.

An electrified treadle is not always a good deal. In the early days of electric sewing machines, many companies produced kits to "electrify" their regular treadle machines. Others, Singer in particular, brought out a line of electric machines that were clearly converted treadles. The factory-installed motor is usually good. If the brand of the motor matches the machine, it is also a good sign. However, beware the "home-handyman" style of electrifying. I've found two machines where the motors weren't appropriate, and they burned out. The old Singers are usually gems, by the way. Try to get one with all its attachments and the original instruction booklet, but don't refuse a machine because these are missing. You can often buy replacements at Singer dealers.

If you aren't going to handsew, and a treadle machine sounds too eccentric, then I recommend a good quality electric machine, and that you take very good care of it. The ultimate is a professional-quality machine, but that depends upon your budget. Talk with friends and professional fabric artists before you put money into any machine. Fancy is not always best.

Assuming that you have a reliable electric machine, take these preliminary steps. First of all, if it hasn't been serviced lately, take it in before you start a major project. If you have a zillion small seams to sew in a pieced bodice and gored skirt, your patience will wear out with frequently breaking threads or a roving tension.

When you pick up your machine, talk with the repair shop. Learn how to keep your machine at its best. My repairman took the time to show me each spot on the machine that should be oiled, and how often I should oil it (in terms of hours spent sewing). For the volume of sewing that I was doing at the time, I needed to oil my machine every second day. He also showed me how to take apart the bobbin housing to clean it. After 5 years, my tension needs work again, but nothing else has caused a problem.

You'll want to have a stack of extra needles on hand, too. Get the best. As a needle starts to get dull, you'll hear a "pop" as it enters the fabric. When you're sewing through several layers of fabric, this becomes important. Don't get frugal at this point. Replace the needle as soon as you even *think* it might be getting dull.

You might want to consider safety glasses (Fig. 3–10). I don't want to frighten you, but I've had two needles break when sewing through multiple layers of fabric. One needle grazed my cheek,

Safety glasses

Fig. 3–10

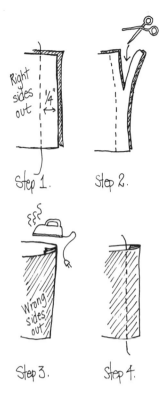

Step 1.

Step 2.

Step 3.

Step 4.

Fig. 3–11

which was quite a scare because it happened so quickly. I've talked with other fabric artists, and it is not uncommon to hear of a needle snapping. Perhaps it gets bent a bit by a slightly-out-of-sync bobbin. Or maybe you push or pull the fabric when you're working on something that needs special care. We've all done that. Or perhaps your needle hits a button or pin during sewing. A few stitches later, the needle is out of line, and it snaps as soon as it hits the plate. If the thread also breaks, the pointed end of the needle can be propelled through the air with alarming speed. This is true of all sewing, not merely historical costuming. Most hardware stores carry a selection of safety glasses. Choose a pair that are really comfortable. Get all those goodies that are designed for regular glasses: nose padding, if you need it, and maybe one of those cords that keeps your glasses around your neck when you take them off for a moment.

Always use the best thread that you can buy. For fine fabrics, especially silks, select an extra-fine machine-embroidery thread (see Resources listing) and a size 10/11 (70) needle for fine fabrics. Always match your thread size to one thread of the fabric. Then choose a needle size to match the thread. If your thread is too fat, your fabric will pucker along the seam.

If this sounds thoroughly confusing — and even if it doesn't — you should read *The Complete Book of Machine Embroidery* by Robbie & Tony Fanning (Chilton, 1986, $16.95). This book explains needles, threads, and sewing machines, with the detail you need for fine quality garments.

Finishing

Handsewing is ideal for finishing, no matter what the era. It's worth repeating: Never use machine topstitching on pre-1890 clothing.

When I sew clothing that I'm going to wear for years, I prefer to use French seams, but that means sewing each seam twice (Fig. 3–11). First, stitch with a ¼″ seam allowance, *wrong* sides together. Trim the seam allowance to ⅛″. Then press the seam to one side and fold one side over the other, so that the raw edges are encased between the right sides. Stitch another ¼″ seam line, just as you ordinarily would. If you didn't trim your seams well enough, unraveling threads will peek through the new seam. Also, certain seams are physically impossible to successfully turn for a French

You Can Sew Your Own Reproductions

seam. Think it through logically, rather than rip out an unsuccessful seam.

Now is the time to use all those wonderful finishing techniques you learned in Advanced Tailoring class, or in books on sewing (see especially Claire Shaeffer's under References). Of course, you won't use a technique that is visibly more modern than the time period you're representing. Remember that this garment will probably last for years, and you'll feel extra proud if you've used your best finishing techniques on it. Sew your Colonial buttonholes by hand. Apply beading to your 1920s gown. Use perspiration pads under the arms of your warm-weather garments. These details will make your clothing extra special.

Colonial country garb. Photo courtesy of Colonial Williamsburg Foundation, Audio-Visual Dept.

SEWING AND COLLECTING VINTAGE FASHIONS

Colonial bum roll

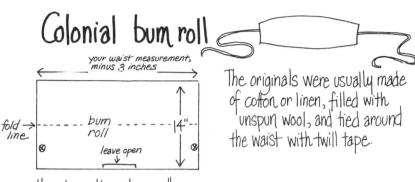

your waist measurement,
minus 3 inches

fold line →

bum roll

14"

leave open

The originals were usually made of cotton or linen, filled with unspun wool, and tied around the waist with twill tape.

How to make a bum roll:

Cut 2 pieces of twill tape or ribbon, each 12" long. Sew each to the bum roll at the ⊗ on the pattern. Fold fabric in half and sew ends closed. Sew closed along widest edge, leaving center open to stuff. Turn bum roll right side out, stuff with wool, batting, or fabric scraps. (Do not stuff too much - roll must remain flexible.) Close edge.

Victorian bustle

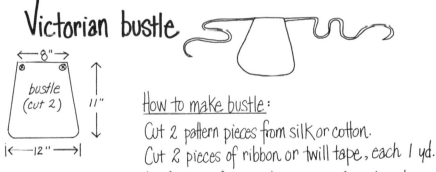

8"

bustle
(cut 2)

11"

12"

How to make bustle:

Cut 2 pattern pieces from silk or cotton.
Cut 2 pieces of ribbon or twill tape, each 1 yd.

Sew ribbons on wrong side of bustle fabric, at ⊗ marks (one at each mark, on one bustle piece). Place two bustle pieces together, right sides facing each other. Sew along outside edge, leaving open at top to stuff. Turn right side out and stuff with batting. Do not overstuff – it should be as soft as a bed pillow. Fold top edges in and sew to finish edge.

Fig. 3–12

Colonial pocket

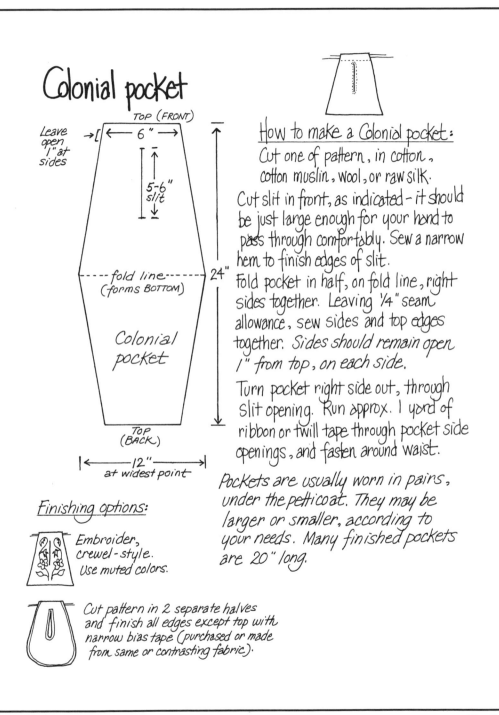

Leave open 1" at sides →⌐

TOP (FRONT)

← 6" →

5-6" slit

--- fold line --- (forms BOTTOM)

24"

Colonial pocket

TOP (BACK)

|← 12" →| at widest point

Finishing options:

Embroider, crewel-style. Use muted colors.

Cut pattern in 2 separate halves and finish all edges except top with narrow bias tape (purchased or made from same or contrasting fabric).

How to make a Colonial pocket:

Cut one of pattern, in cotton, cotton muslin, wool, or raw silk.

Cut slit in front, as indicated – it should be just large enough for your hand to pass through comfortably. Sew a narrow hem to finish edges of slit.

Fold pocket in half, on fold line, right sides together. Leaving ¼" seam allowance, sew sides and top edges together. *Sides should remain open 1" from top, on each side.*

Turn pocket right side out, through slit opening. Run approx. 1 yard of ribbon or twill tape through pocket side openings, and fasten around waist.

Pockets are usually worn in pairs, under the petticoat. They may be larger or smaller, according to your needs. Many finished pockets are 20" long.

Fig. 3–13

Mob cap

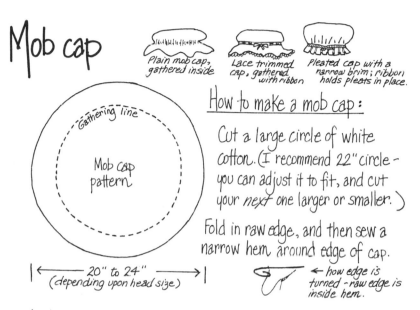

Plain mob cap, gathered inside

Lace trimmed cap, gathered with ribbon

Pleated cap with a narrow brim; ribbon holds pleats in place.

Gathering line

Mob cap pattern

|← 20" to 24" →|
(depending upon head size)

How to make a mob cap:

Cut a large circle of white cotton. (I recommend 22" circle - you can adjust it to fit, and cut your *next* one larger or smaller.)

Fold in raw edge, and then sew a narrow hem around edge of cap.

← how edge is turned - raw edge is inside hem.

Handsewing is recommended for the hem. If you iron the folds into the hem first, it takes about an hour (in front of the tv) to sew the hem by hand. (The entire cap can be handmade in an evening.)

The cap is then gathered, about 2" from the hem. You can sew a casing along this line (dotted line on pattern) inside the cap, and then run a ribbon through it, and tie it so that the cap fits. Or you can measure some elastic to the correct size, gather the cap to fit the elastic, and sew the elastic inside the cap. Or you can sew some cutwork- type trim along the gathering line, on the outside of the cap. Then run a ribbon through the trim, gathering the cap to fit, and tie the ribbon in a pretty bow. (There are _many_ other options.)

Lace trim can be used to decorate the cap. This is especially nice when the cap is worn under a straw bonnet.

Fig. 3-14

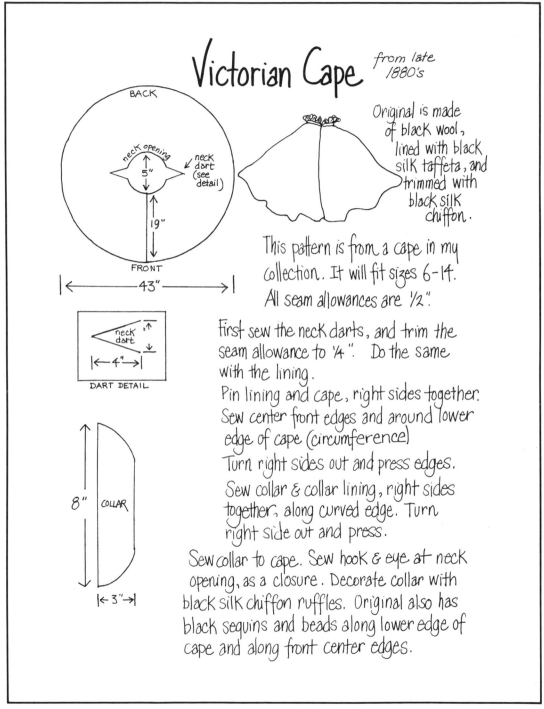

Victorian Cape

from late 1880's

BACK

neck opening

neck dart (see detail)

5"

19"

FRONT

|←——— 43" ———→|

neck dart

|←— 4" —→|

DART DETAIL

8" COLLAR

|← 3" →|

Original is made of black wool, lined with black silk taffeta, and trimmed with black silk chiffon.

This pattern is from a cape in my collection. It will fit sizes 6-14. All seam allowances are ½".

First sew the neck darts, and trim the seam allowance to ¼". Do the same with the lining.

Pin lining and cape, right sides together. Sew center front edges and around lower edge of cape (circumference)

Turn right sides out and press edges.

Sew collar & collar lining, right sides together, along curved edge. Turn right side out and press.

Sew collar to cape. Sew hook & eye at neck opening, as a closure. Decorate collar with black silk chiffon ruffles. Original also has black sequins and beads along lower edge of cape and along front center edges.

Fig. 3-15

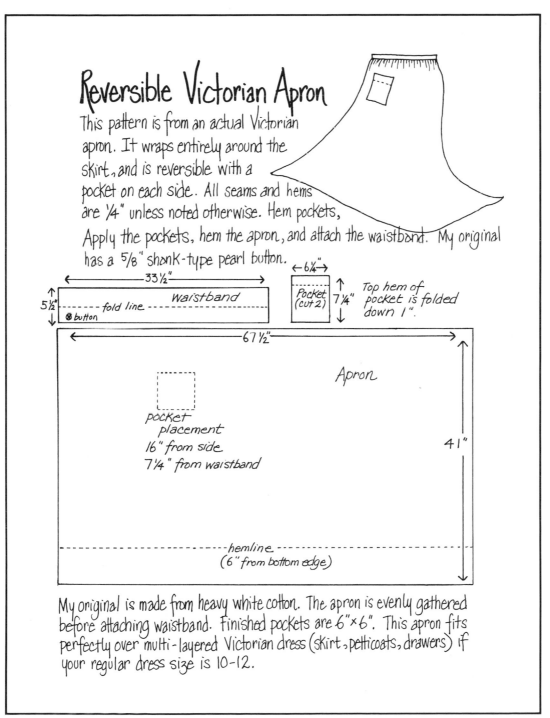

Reversible Victorian Apron

This pattern is from an actual Victorian apron. It wraps entirely around the skirt, and is reversible with a pocket on each side. All seams and hems are ¼" unless noted otherwise. Hem pockets, Apply the pockets, hem the apron, and attach the waistband. My original has a ⅝" shank-type pearl button.

← 33½" →

Waistband

5½" -- fold line --

⊗ button

← 6¼" →

Pocket (cut 2)

7¼"

Top hem of pocket is folded down 1".

← 67½" →

Apron

pocket placement
16" from side
7¼" from waistband

41"

hemline
(6" from bottom edge)

My original is made from heavy white cotton. The apron is evenly gathered before attaching waistband. Finished pockets are 6"×6". This apron fits perfectly over multi-layered Victorian dress (skirt, petticoats, drawers) if your regular dress size is 10-12.

Fig. 3–16

CHAPTER 4

Shortcuts
or, "How Accurate
Does This Have To Be?"

When you're making a costume for a party, for an amateur play, or for some other quick-in-a-hurry event, you don't need perfection. If it conveys the general historical idea, you're all set. That's what we'll talk about in this chapter. However, you should read Chapter 3 to learn about selecting patterns, materials, colors, and to glean tips on making clothing. Often, you'll start with the shortcuts, but add some dramatic touches to make your costume special. *All* of these suggestions will make purists turn pale in horror. None are intended to convey an accurate historical image. These are for *fun*, such as Halloween or murder mystery parties, and similar occasions.

First, I recommend that you locate the paperback book, *Costume 1066–1966* by John Peacock (published by Thames and Hudson, NY), I found my copy in the Museum of Fine Arts gift shop, in Boston. The book is almost entirely illustrations, with notes on important fashion details covering nearly every era.

Renaissance Fair,
by Larry Brazil.

Fig. 4-1

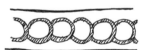

Fig. 4-2

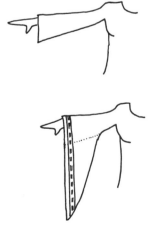

Fig. 4-3

MEDIEVAL COSTUMES

Women's Garments

For a woman's costume, a trip to the attic or to the local thrift shop may produce the exact gown you need. Many of the long dresses worn in the 1960s and early 70s are simple enough to mimic Medieval tunics (Fig. 4–1). Look for a muted color. If the dress is bright, such as day-glo pink, use fabric dye to soften the color. If you're a novice at using dyes, a grocery store brand such as Rit will be fine. You can get involved with more precise dyes, such as PROcion and Ciba, but since we're talking shortcuts here, I'm assuming that you want the easiest dye that you can find.

Next, you may want to add a wide, embroidered border for elegance. If you select a design, it should be something geometric rather than cute little duckies (see examples of appropriate motifs in Fig. 4–2).

Make a simple veil from an oval piece of fabric, adding a headband to hold it in place. The final touch to your costume will be a cord, suede, fabric, or macrame belt that rests on the hips.

If you want something fancier, widen the sleeves with triangle-shaped inserts, so that the sleeves are belled (Fig. 4–3). Finish the edges with an embroidered trim.

The over-tunic/under-tunic look is one of the most spectacular for this era (Fig. 4–4). You can remove the sleeves of the dress entirely, and then deepen the armholes. Wear this over a long-sleeved, solid color, traditional leotard (not the shiny kind). Or you can shorten the sleeves rather than remove them, and take up the hem so it is just below your knees. Under this, wear a floor-length gown with long, fitted sleeves. In other words, you'll be wearing two gowns, with the shorter one on top. Or you can wear a long-sleeve traditional leotard and a skirt in a matching color. Under the over-tunic, these will look like one piece.

For an elaborate hat, find an old pillbox felt hat, strip off any trim, and add fake jewels around the crown. It may be necessary to shorten the hat a bit if the crown is too high. Push down the top of the hat a bit and see if you can hide its original height; if you trim off the bottom, it will stretch too much without a grosgrain ribbon inside. Drape a fabric well over or under this hat (Fig. 4–5). For who-cares costume party wear, you can dye a sailor's hat with the brim turned up, glue jewels or gaudy trim on it, and wear a veil over the crown so that only the front band is revealed.

Fig. 4–4

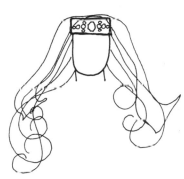

Fig. 4–5

1960's dress..... becomes a man's tunic

Fig. 4–6

Men's Clothing

A good, heavy pair of tights is the first item for a generic Medieval man's costume. See if he can wear your darkest opaque tights. If they're too revealing, go to the dance supply store and buy *real* men's dance tights. You can often order these through stores such as Parklane.

Next, he'll need a pair of boots or slippers. Leather moccasins, without the fringe and fancy trim, are pretty good. Pointy toes were in fashion, so avoid really round toes if possible. On the other hand, don't use Western boots, even if the toes are pointy. The simplest leather boots are the best. Again, you may find what you need at the thrift shop. But clean them thoroughly with a disinfectant to prevent athlete's foot and plantar's warts.

While you're at the thrift shop, pick up a second 1960s-style dress for him. Follow the same guidelines as for the women's gown, above. Obviously, select brown, black, forest green, or some other "male" color. If you can't find the right color, you'll need fabric dye for this, too. And don't buy a dress with bust or waist darts!

If you can't find a gown, try the bathrobe section of the thrift shop. Sometimes a robe can be trimmed and sewed to make a convincing tunic.

Whatever garment you start with, trim it so that the hem falls somewhere between calf and mid-thigh when the tunic is belted (Fig. 4–6). The belt you select will be like a woman's (described above), but wider.

Before you leave the thrift shop, look for old fur pieces. Shabby ones are okay as long as they aren't too ratty; be certain that they don't have a foul odor, since they will be worn near the face. Fake fur is fine, if it is fairly convincing.

Check for a plain blanket, bedspread, or tablecloth that can become a cloak. For the cloak, select a piece of fabric that is at least 45" square. In fact, select the largest size that you might possibly need, and you can trim it down. Trim a little here and a little there, experimenting, until you have a cloak you like. On a large man, a cloak 55" by 60" will flow beautifully as he walks. The wide horizontal dimension allows him to tie the cloak to fasten it, rather than using a pin. If he uses a pin, select something authentic

Shortcuts or, "How Accurate Does This Have To Be?"

Fig. 4–7

from a source such as Raymond's Quiet Press (see Resources section), or use a plain, round scarf pin.

The fur pieces can be basted as a collar (leaving enough top edge to tie, of course), or draped over one shoulder dramatically.

His costume is now complete, except for a hat. Personally, I'd skip a hat entirely, since there is no easy Medieval man's hat. If you must have one, check with local costume shops to rent one.

ELIZABETHAN WEAR

Women's Garments

The correct Elizabethan look includes a perfectly flat chest. If you want to try this and you're just too shapely au naturel, use Ace bandages to bind your chest. Be sensible about this; you don't want discomfort, and you'll need to be able to breathe. An alternative might be one of the older styles of sports bras, which also flatten the breasts. (Thrift shops and yard sales are good places to find these.) If you can't stand either of these choices, then you'll have to unfashionably shapely.

Your gown can be made or purchased in two parts. The blouse should fit like skin and have a collarless square or oval neckline. (You can always strip the collar off and turn the edges in as a hem.) Any sleeve is fine. A leotard is too figure-revealing for this; it must be a blouse. The skirt should match in color, but it will be floor-length and very, very full. A hem circumference of 150″ is reasonable. If you're making the blouse, add a ruffle of the same fabric around the bottom edge of the blouse, which will be worn outside the skirt. The ruffle can be as deep as 12″.

Inside the neck of the blouse, use a sheer fabric that fills the opening, all the way to the collarbone. Gauzy fabric of any kind is fine. Baste this in place. Hemming is unnecessary. Use a simple running stitch to gather it at the neckline. Then add a ruff collar, which isn't as difficult as it looks (Fig. 4–7).

To make a ruff collar, start with two circles of fabric that you'll cut together to make two identical pieces. Cut them in a spiral, with the cutaway portion being slightly larger than the depth of your planned collar (Fig. 4–8). I recommend practicing with paper until you have the sizes planned to meet your needs. After cut-

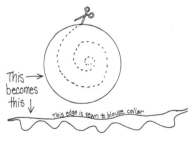

This → becomes this ↓

This edge is sewn to blouse collar

Fig. 4–8

ting, place right sides together and seam them along the wider, outside edge. Press the seam allowance open. Then trim the seam allowance and fold the two layers right-side-out. When you lay the collar on a straight line, the outer edges will buckle nicely, giving you a head start on your collar. Then you need to tack the collar as you loosely fold it up and down, to achieve the ruff you want. The final step is to use bias seam binding to finish the inside edge of the collar, and leave long enough ends on the binding so that you can use them to tie the collar on. If you make the collar to fit your neck precisely, you'll find that it soon feels uncomfortably snug.

An alternative to the ruff collar is to leave the neckline open and add a standing collar at the back (Fig. 4–9). Measure the circumference of the neckline; that will be the bottom (inside) measurement of the collar (Fig. 4–10). You'll cut it with a gradual slope, but the top should measure no more than a few inches larger than the neckline edge. An it can be up to 8″ tall, adding about ½″ for your seam.

At the fabric store, buy the fabric for the collar (double your dimensions, for the inside and outside of the collar). Also buy a piece of fusible interfacing, in the size of the finished collar. I recommend buying the heavy stuff that is intended for making window shades. If you can't find that, buy the heaviest, stiffest fusible interfacing that they have, or fuse two more layers on top of each other.

While you're at the fabric store, pick up ribbon, lace, and pearl trim to add flair to your outfit. Look for readymade cuffs or material for creating nice deep, stiff cuffs for your blouse. Ideally, your cuffs should match your collar.

Your next stop is a large crafts supply shop, such as Lee Wards. For the collar, you'll need some nice, heavy wire. Florist's wire will do, as long as it holds a shape fairly well. Stay away from wire that melts easily, because you'll be ironing this. That's why I do not recommend soldering wire, although it is often the ideal stiffness.

Before you leave the crafts shop, you should select some feathers. Choose fluffy feathers, about 2″ long, lots of them. They should match your gown or complement it. Buy about 3 yards of satin ribbon or thin, shiny cord, to match the feathers.

Your final purchase is a wooden spoon. Select the cheapest one, because only the handle will show.

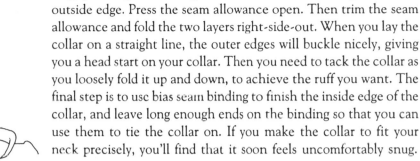

Fig. 4–9

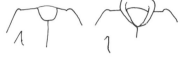

Fig. 4–10

Shortcuts or, "How Accurate Does This Have To Be?"

When you arrive home, first cut the pieces of your collar. You'll be making your own pattern for this, so keep fitting it to the blouse to be certain it is the right size. Follow the guidelines I described earlier. You may want a wider seam allowance, to help support the collar.

Once you have the fabric cut to size, cut one piece of the fusible interfacing, the size of the finished collar. In other words, it shouldn't overlap the lines where you'll be sewing. Between the weight of the interfacing and its glue-like surface, your sewing machine may balk.

Next, prepare to cut the wire. Use wire clippers or your oldest scissors for this. Your sewing scissors will be damaged if you use them for wire cutting.

Cut one piece of wire to follow the edges of the finished collar. Then, depending upon the height of your collar, you may need a few extra vertical supports to hold up the back (Fig. 4–11). Remember: Your collar is going to stand straight up.

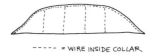

Fig. 4–11

Your next step is to *carefully* fuse the interfacing to the wrong side of one piece of your collar. The wire will be *between* the interfacing and the collar, and you'll be sealing it into little tunnels inside. This is why you should be careful. If the wire is easily melted, you might have a fried collar!

Finally, finish the collar as you ordinarily would. Sew wrong sides together and then turn it right-side-out, to attach inside the neckline of the garment.

Now you're ready to complete your costume.

You'll be adding as much trim as you can, in the time and budget you have allowed. I recommend checking *Costume 1066–1966* for ideas. Sleeves, bodices, necklines, waistlines—all are places for jewels, rows of lace, and ribbons.

Accessories can make all the difference in a costume. A fan adds style and it is easy to make with feathers, ribbon, a piece of cardboard, and a wooden spoon.

Take the wooden spoon, and glue fan-shaped cardboard on either side of it, leaving about 6″ of handle sticking out (Fig. 4–12). Cover one side of the fan cardboard with white glue, and stick on mountains of the fluffy feathers that you bought. When that side dries, turn the fan over and glue feathers on the other side. A final touch is to tie the 3 yards of cord or ribbon to the handle of the spoon. Place the spoon handle at the midpoint of the ribbon, and tie the knot there. Secure the spoon to the ribbon with a drop

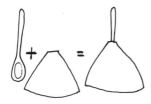

Fig. 4–12

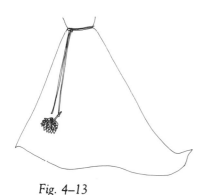

Fig. 4–13

of white glue. About 15" or 20" from where it was tied to the spoon, tie a knot holding the two pieces of ribbon together. The remaining ends are tied around your waist once the costume is complete (Fig. 4–13). You may have to shorten it a bit, if the fan touches the ground. However, it can hang anywhere between waist and hem. You can glue some jewels on the handle of the fan, for extra effect.

If you prefer, you can skip the fan and tie a small round hand mirror to the ribbon or cord. The problem here will be covering the plastic on the mirror. You can use white glue and fabric, or lots of jewels, or both. Obviously, they did not have plastic in Elizabethan times.

Another nice accessory is a hat. Your hat can be a long triangle of lace with the point to the front. Or you can wear a simple veil. A beanie-style cap is also nice and Shakespearean. Think *Romeo and Juliet*.

The final touch will be ropes of pearls. Pearls were *the* fashion accessory of the 1590s. You can find these at the discount store, at yard sales, or at the thrift shop. If you buy a string of pearls with some chipped beads, take a hammer and smash the chipped ones so that they fall off the string. If the string is worn, this won't work, because the string will break and it won't be worth restringing them. An alternative is to get a silver or gold feltwriter at the crafts store or a large stationery shop. Use that to color the beads that are chipped, peeling, or stained. Not all beads will accept paint, so don't invest a lot of money in supplies to color chipped beads.

The basic costume is completed, but you should consider one more item for a spectacular effect: a bum roll. This is a large, padded tube that encircled the waist under the gown, and supported the skirt. The easiest shortcut is to use the carry-all that is designed for skiers, and fastens around the waist like a belt. Stuff it with tissue or pillowcases, and it is ready to wear. If you don't have access to a carry-all, sew a nice big tube of cloth, stuff it with batting, old pantyhose, or any other convenient, lightweight stuffing, and sew a long ribbon at each end when you complete it. Before you complete it, be certain that the stuffing is all at the back and sides of your body when the bum roll is on. Women were relatively flat-stomached in Elizabethan times. After you finish sewing, tie the ribbons around your waist, and you have a nearly authentic bum roll.

Shortcuts or, "How Accurate Does This Have To Be?"

Fig. 4–14

If you choose to wear a bum roll, wear a slip or petticoat over it, or it will look like a strange bulge under your skirt. If your regular slip isn't big enough, you can pick up wearable Victorian slips. Buy the least expensive one you can — who cares if it has been repaired a few dozen times? Or borrow a square-dancing petticoat from a country friend.

Men's Apparel

Again, you're going to start with nice, heavy tights. They must be opaque since there will be a lot of leg showing. Next, you need to decide if he's going to wear trunks or just a tunic.

Trunks are historically accurate, but they can look really ridiculous. Basically, they look like bloomers (Fig. 4–14). Use any shorts pattern, cut the legs and waistline extra wide to have fabric to gather, and skip the fly front. Run elastic through the waist and at the cuffs. Stuff the legs and hips of these trunks with tissue paper, if he won't be sitting down. In Elizabethan times, they were stuffed with horsehair.

Breeches came into fashion toward the end of Elizabeth's reign. Make these from regular pants that you cut off, as long as the fly front and belt loops are covered by the doublet or tunic. Cut the pants so they reach just below the knee when hemmed. Gather them with ribbons that are tied similar to old-time garters.

Either of these can be worn with a doublet — a jacket that has been tailored to fit closely, like an extremely tapered shirt. Only dartless, pocketless suit jackets can be used for this. Taper it at the side seams, rather than with darts. Again, a man's bathrobe may be your best choice if you aren't making it from scratch.

A padded roll, about the size of a dinner sausage, should be tacked on at the shoulder seam. This goes outside the doublet, not inside.

An alternative to the doublet is a tunic. A tunic is not particularly accurate, but most people think of tunics as part of that era, and they look like a million dollars on most men. Actually, they date to Henry VIII. Use *Costumes 1066–1966*, and the ideas covered under Medieval men's costuming. Your tunic/doublet should be much shorter than the one I described in that section.

A ruff, similar to the one described in Elizabethan women's fashions, is a nice accent.

Fig. 4–15

Shoes can be leather slippers or scuffs, ballet slippers, or even cotton slippers from China.

For a hat, select the cheapest felt hat you can find. The brim needs to be trimmed to about 2″. The crown will be covered with gathered fabric. Cut a large circle of fabric that will cover the crown down to where it meets the brim. Use white glue to fasten the fabric in place, with masking tape or pins to hold the fabric until it dries. Then cover the edges of the fabric with a ribbon that ties around the hat. Finally, stick a nice, full feather in the ribbon, as decoration (Fig. 4–15).

His costume will look only as impressive as he feels in it. Tell him to walk like a pirate. Pirates were in their glory during the Elizabethan era.

AMERICAN COLONIAL COSTUMES

Women's Fashions

As we approach modern day fashions, it becomes easier to "improvise" quick costumes.

For a country woman, you'll need a peasant blouse, also called a Mexican blouse, because that's where the best ones are made. It should have no decorations whatsoever. Long sleeves are important, so that you can push them up to just below your elbow. Short sleeves weren't worn, though you can get away with them if this is for a costume party. With this blouse, wear a full, floor-length skirt in a plain, muted color. At your neck, wear a large, solid-color kerchief crossed in the front and tucked into your blouse. You may have to safety-pin this in place, but conceal the safety pin. Instead of pins, Colonial women often used thorns. If you want to be that accurate, be prepared for the damage that thorns will do to your fabric.

As with all costuming, the accessories are important to the total look. In Colonial costuming in particular, people expect to see certain items.

On your head, wear a mob cap (Fig. 4–16). This is the most important item to convey the idea of Colonial America. Some mail-order shops sell these so inexpensively that it's hardly worth taking the time to sew one. However, if you don't have the time to

Shortcuts or, "How Accurate Does This Have To Be?"

Fig. 4–16

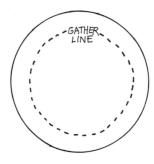

Fig. 4–17

order one, use the pattern provided in Fig. 3–14 or follow these easy instructions: Cut a large circle of fabric, up to 22" across. Hem the edges. Cut a piece of elastic that will fit comfortably around your head. Sew this in a circle, about 2" in from the hem (Fig. 4–17). Sew a little ribbon bow on the outside at the front center, if you want some decoration. An authentic mob cap would have a casing instead of the elastic, with a ribbon pulled through it and tied on the outside front, to adjust the fit. It takes so little extra work to sew an authentic cap, it's almost worth making one. However, if you're hemming your cap with the sewing machine, it won't be authentic anyway, so go ahead and use elastic. You may choose to apply a casing and run the elastic through that, for extra comfort. Another choice is to zigzag stitch over ⅛" ribbon or elastic, and then pull the ribbon to gather it.

Another accurate hat is a straw hat with silk flowers on the brim. Tie a ribbon over it to hold it down. You may need to tack the ribbon in place here and there. You can turn the back of the brim up, for a special effect. The look is similar to an Aussie hat, but sideways. You wear this *over* the mob cap, which peeks out all around.

A shawl is a good idea if the weather is cool. A cape made from a blanket is an alternative for chilly weather. Make it as simple as possible, or just wrap it around your shoulders. Your blanket should not have finished edges. If it does, and the blanket is a permanent part of your costume wardrobe, cut the edges off the blanket. A thermal blanket is not correct: use cotton or woolen blankets in muted color.

Footwear is less important during this era. Your shoes can be plain leather pumps in black or brown. Your stockings can be white. In hot weather, wear knee socks; no one will know the difference, and you'll be cooler. If you cannot find cotton knee socks in the women's department, buy men's cotton knee socks. Their support socks are most comfortable.

If you are pretending to be someone from the countryside, there are a couple of items you can easily add to your costume. First, a belt of cotton cording is practical. Before a woman went shopping for sewing supplies, she would take a cord and tie knots in it, representing measurements of the person she was shopping for. The distance between two knots might represent how long her husband's shirt should be, or the total length of a dress for a child.

On the belt, you might wear a tin cup. It was a nice luxury for a woman to have when she was traveling. When she stopped at someone's well for water, she could use her own cup rather than share with the other travelers.

The final touch is to carry a reproduction pistol. Some inexpensive ones don't actually fire, and are a good choice. If you want to look like an independent Colonial woman rather than her frail counterpart, a pistol conveys the idea instantly.

Fig. 4–18

With some extra work, you can "graduate" to a more formal look. For a more elaborate Colonial gown, add another skirt. If you start with a readymade skirt, it should be very full and in a color that complements the first skirt. Slit the new skirt up the middle to the waistband (leave the waistband intact). Hem these newly cut edges. Take the points of the front and safety pin them inside the skirt, toward the back of the waistband (Fig. 4–18). Adjust until you achieve the look you want. It's like balloon curtains, in effect. This is worn over the first skirt.

Choose a blouse that is the same color as the overskirt. It should be simple, collarless, with a wide-open neckline, and it should cover your elbows. No cuffs, either. You could dye a peasant blouse to match the underskirt. Tuck a large kerchief in at the neckline. The kerchief should be white, and it can be lace-trimmed. It is worn as described in the simpler Colonial woman's costume.

Of course, for all the trouble of matching blouses and skirts and making alterations, it might be just as easy to use the Pegee of Williamsburg pattern. Mine took less than a day to make, and I love it. Obviously, I made the simplest version. I have a small bustline, so I left out the darts, and it fits perfectly.

Fig. 4–19

Men's Garb

Choose any white or cream-colored shirt, as long as it is simple with full, bloused sleeves (Fig. 4–19). A pullover style shirt is preferred. The collar should be soft and unstarched. Inside the shirt, at the neck, you an use a white silk woman's tie, the sort that is sold at the scarf counter in stores. You can also use a long, full, dark silk tie; a skinny, dark little tie is going to look ridiculous. Think in terms of a cravat. Otherwise, skip the tie altogether.

His breeches are made the same as the Elizabethan men's breeches, except that you'll prefer a white or buff color for them.

65

Chinos or light-colored khakis are great. Black and navy are acceptable, too. Run an elastic through the hem, instead of using the ribbon garter I mentioned earlier.

Next, he should wear a vest. If you have a long vest that covers him to mid-thigh, no one will see the fly front and belt loops on his improvised breeches. Select a dark-colored vest and keep it buttoned.

If you're going to have to sew a vest to cover the fly on the breeches, consider skipping the long vest and make an authentic pair of breeches instead. I've used the breeches pattern from Eagles View (see Resources) with excellent results, though I had to read the instructions carefully to construct the drop front. Over that went a straight, simple, long cotton vest that I bought second-hand.

His socks should be white or should match his breeches. The best are men's support hose in kneesock length. They have enough elastic to keep from falling down. Women's knee socks are usually too small, and roll down easily. The socks can go over or under the edge of the breeches. It is more comfortable to wear them under, but the socks can be used to cover an unfinished edge on the breeches, and still be historically correct.

For shoes, choose any black or brown plain loafer. Penny loafers and most tie shoes look too modern. For around $10 you can buy a perfectly good plain loafer at the discount store. They may not be comfortable enough for regular wear, but for costume use, they're better than penny loafers.

There is no substitute for a tricorn, but you can make one yourself in a pinch. Find a black floppy felt hat. Again, we're talking 1960s and 70s, and thrift shops. Trim the brim as necessary, and tack it with black thread so that the brim is lifted up on three sides. You can do the same with a large-brimmed straw hat. The effect isn't as clearly Colonial as the black felt, but it is still moderately accurate.

If tricorns are beyond you, then a plain, knitted ski cap is also from the Colonial era. If you can use a contrasting shade of yarn and hastily stitch on the word "Liberty," you'll have a cap that is quite authentic.

REGENCY COSTUMES

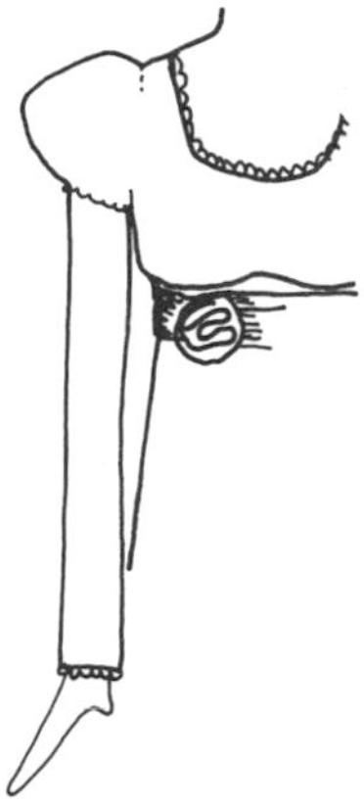

Women's Wear

It can be so difficult to find the right, empire-style gown to remodel for Regency wear that I'm tempted to tell you to skip this and make the Pegee gown for that era.

Fig. 4–20

You must find a gown that has the waistline right under the bust. If you *do* find one, chances are that it will have the correct, puffed sleeves of the time. Simply add long, fitted undersleeves (Fig. 4–20), and some decoration around the hem. Sometimes you can find the right style in the bridal section of thrift shops. Nightgowns are often in this design, but you may have difficulty finding one in a fabric that doesn't look like a nightgown.

Use a sash at the dress's waistline. Select a pastel fabric for this, and buy silk if possible. For such a small piece, the price will be low and the effect will be dazzling.

Once you have the basic gown, select accessories. The gowns were so simple during that era, you'll need to add these extras for a finished look.

A parasol is a nice addition, but it must have a long handle, like a walking stick. Try to rent one at a costume shop. If you can't, don't waste your time trying to rig one up with an umbrella. The handles are too different.

Long shawls were worn as much for decoration as for cool weather. The best place to find an appropriate shawl is at your grandmother's house. Table runners are often the exact dimensions you need.

A hat is vital, unless your hair can be styled as they did during that era. Your straw hat can be as simple as taking an oval straw placemat, running a ribbon across it that will tie under your chin, and then placing many silk flowers on the top. Try on the placemats for the correct size. Do this with a scarf on, or you'll upset the store clerks who don't want hair oil on their merchandise. (Yes, you're going to feel ridiculous putting on a placemat, and I have no easy solution for this problem.) If the placemats are all too large, you can always trim one down and then glue ribbon over the raw edges.

Otherwise, a poke bonnet is correct, particularly with a flattering lining of silk and/or silk flowers around the face. It should have a short brim so that your face is not entirely hidden.

Shortcuts or, "How Accurate Does This Have To Be?"

Ballet slippers are fine for shoes. Small fabric slippers are also great. Find these for a few dollars a pair in a department store. They're sold as travel slippers and usually come in a small plastic pouch.

Men's Costumes

Unfortunately, drop-front pants were still the fashion, and there is no good way to disguise contemporary pants. You can sew the drop-front pants or rent them from a costume shop. Or you can forget accuracy entirely in this case. After all, it's only a costume.

His jacket should be a cutaway tuxedo jacket, with tails. Wide lapels are ideal, so look in thrift shops for tuxedos from the late 1960s. Single- and double-breasted jackets are equally acceptable.

A vest is a nice accessory. Look for a fairly ornate short vest in thrift shops. If he'll be keeping his jacket on, you can cut the shape of a vest front from upholstery fabric, stitch on a few nice golden buttons and a mock hem, and then safety pin this to his shirt, where the pins won't show. This is a shortcut that I have used successfully for costume parties.

His shirt should be white and ruffled if possible. Again, you'll find affordable ruffled shirts in thrift shops, in the same section as the tuxedos. If he'll keep his vest on, stains on the shirt won't show. If he'll keep his jacket on, you can even have stained or torn sleeves, and it won't matter. Never buy a garment that is fancier and more expensive than you need.

At the neck, he should wear a full cravat. It should be the long kind, wrapped around his throat a couple of times, and then tied in a full bow in front.

The correct hat is a tall-crowned top hat with a very curled brim. This can be impossible to find outside of a costume shop, so don't waste time searching.

Toward the end of the Regency, men began wearing frock coats. You can find these in some thrift shops. They were worn throughout the nineteenth century, and into the early twentieth century. A correct frock coat will fit like skin. Men had valets to help them get in and out of these coats. Basically, they're similar to regular coats but they are knee-length, and full like a skirt in the back. If he wears a frock coat and keeps it buttoned, you don't have to worry about the fly front on the pants showing. However, frock coats are often warmer than you'd expect. He's not likely to keep it buttoned at an indoor event.

Any dress shoes are fine, as long as they are the type that slip on. Shoes that tie are not correct.

VICTORIAN AND CIVIL WAR ERA APPAREL

Women's Costumes

This is another era for which you need to browse through the pictures in a costume book. If you use a book that shows actual photos of that time, you'll see the important details you should have in your costume.

Fig. 4-21

Dresses were huge, with yards and yards of fabric. Prom gowns are your best choice, though you may have to dye one to a more appropriate color. If you're simply dyeing the fabric black or a very dark shade, you might be able to use Rit. Otherwise, learn to use professional-quality dyes such as PROcion and Ciba (see Resources list).

When selecting your gown, think in terms of *Gone with the Wind*. If the sleeves are completely ridiculous for the Civil War, plan to wear a short cape over your gown. You can often find these in thrift shops, among bathrobes and bed jackets. (If it is a synthetic fabric, don't try to dye it.)

Underneath your gown, you really should have a hoop skirt. For one-time wear, see if you can rent one at a costume shop. It's a fairly common item. Otherwise, check with your local chapter of the Victorian Society to locate a nearby source.

Accessories are equally important for an authentic Victorian impression. Think about the overdone interiors that often represent the Victorian era: heavy fabrics, dark colors, and lots of extra, unnecessary items such as photos, clocks, and Boston ferns. The effect you should create with your clothing is similar. Overdressed will say "Victorian" far more than an austere costume.

Your hair will be an important part of the impression you create. If your hair is short, you should wear a bonnet to cover it. These were generally large, poke-style bonnets (Fig. 4-21).

If your hair is at least chin length and you cannot manage to make or buy a bonnet, buy a snood. This is one of those hairnets that scoop up your hair in the back, but the net doesn't reach far above the tops of your ears in the back. You can buy these in some beauty supply shops, in stores such as Woolworth's if they cater to the older crowd, and sometimes in shops that carry uniforms for nurses. If you have to buy a white one, you can easily dye it to match your gown. I bought some jet buttons at a flea market. Then I put a bobby pin through the shank of each and use those to hold my snood in place. Jet jewelry was popular in Victorian years.

Dangle earrings are appropriate, particularly those made from glass beads (not paste jewelry), pearls, and delicate goldwork.

Shoes are still slippers for evening wear. Follow the recommendations for the Regency.

Men's Clothing

For our purposes, there were few changes in men's fashions between the Regency and the Civil War. The quick Regency costume described above is close enough to Civil War era clothing to be acceptable at a costume party.

What are the important differences between the Regency and the Civil War? The cutaway tux was no longer in fashion, and frock coats were most popular. Ties were smaller, more closely resembling today's bow ties. In fact, if you tie it yourself, you can use a contemporary bow tie. It will be tied over the collar, which should be standing up. If you use a 1970s dress shirt with a short collar, this can work well.

A vest is a vital part of menswear, and it should be ornate, such as a brocade. Upholstery fabric is ideal.

If you prefer to buy a suit, you may find what you need at the thrift shop.

Sack suits were starting to become popular, and had jackets that were similar to leisure suits of recent years. The front corners of the jacket were rounded. Pants were not as figure-revealing as during the Regency. Avoid costumes that show fly fronts and belt loops. It's still too early for them. A vest is a vital part of this costume, too.

Men's hats were round-topped in this era, such as a bowler, and shoes were still slippers and boots; there were no tie shoes.

TWENTIETH-CENTURY COSTUMES

From the Victorian era forward, it is easy to locate costumes and wearables, and to improvise from your own closet, if you know what the fashions looked like. I recommend that you use a costume book (see References section) and that you check local stores in the following Yellow Page categories: Antiques, Clothing; Clothing, Second-Hand; Collectibles; Costumes; Men's Apparel, Used; Second-Hand Shops; Thrift Shops; Women's Apparel, Used. Happy improvisation!

Historical romance authors; from left, Jennifer Blake, Janelle Taylor, and Rosemary Rogers. Photo courtesy of Romantic Times Publishing Group.

Shortcuts or, "How Accurate Does This Have To Be?"

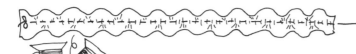

CHAPTER 5

Alterations and Adjustments

Until the twentieth century, people didn't throw away clothing just because it didn't fit. Fabric was expensive or in short supply, and sewing took too long to casually throw a garment out. Therefore, this entire chapter can be condensed into this advice: If it doesn't fit, take it in or add fabric, restitch seams, cover the problem with trim and ruffles, or do whatever is necessary to make it fit.

FITTING VINTAGE GARMENTS

The author in a Victorian bustle/overskirt made from an antique silk cape.

First of all, make certain that your garment really doesn't fit. That may sound completely ridiculous, but here's the explanation: Clothing didn't always fit the way our clothes do today.

During periods in the Medieval and Regency eras, sleeves covered the back of the hand (Fig. 5–1). Don't shorten these sleeves if you can learn to move gracefully with them.

Fig. 5–1

In the late Regency and early Victorian eras, the shoulders on women's gowns were dropped to give women the appearance of having extremely sloped shoulders (Fig. 5–2). This makes arm movement awkward at times, but it won't feel so restricted once you're accustomed to it.

Regency and Victorian costs were often so snug that men had to be helped in and out of them. He'll get used to the fit and it will do wonders for his posture. Be certain that he takes off his coat before lifting heavy objects that would cause his back to flex or stretch; there isn't room in a frock coat for that.

Men's Regency collars and women's late Victorian collars were often high, starched, and uncomfortable (Fig. 5–3). You may want to modify these for comfort, but you'll make such a great impression with the authentic collars, it's worth learning to live with the discomfort.

Obviously, women's gowns trailed from era to era. However, in the Victorian years, shorter gowns were often worn when walking outdoors. Likewise, servants wore shorter gowns for heavy or dirty tasks. Your class level and activity may determine whether a gown is too long or too short.

Fig. 5–2

Fashionable women's sleeves were often too tight to allow much movement, especially during the late seventeenth century and parts of the Victorian era. This tight sleeve designated an upper class woman who didn't have to move her arms: her servants did all the work.

By contrast, men's shirts often had enormous sleeves that were actually one-size-fits-all, and adjusted with a snug-fitting cuff. And long tails on men's shirts and women's chemises were sometimes pulled between the legs and tucked into a waistband to simulate underwear.

If you are sewing new clothing, you may want to make the garment hastily, in an inexpensive fabric. Muslin is often on sale, or you might use an old bedsheet. This way, you can try on the garment before you cut your good fabric. You'll be able to see potential fitting problems before they become a headache. In addition, if you make the trial garment from an accurate but affordable fabric, such as plain white cotton, you'll now have *two* historical gowns to wear.

Fig. 5–3

SEWING AND COLLECTING VINTAGE FASHIONS

ALTERING SECOND-HAND CLOTHING

If you're buying a second-hand garment that doesn't fit correctly, you may not have the luxury of simple alterations. If you have determined that the cut of your garment is *not* a whim of fashion, and it really does need altering, there are several approaches.

Taking In

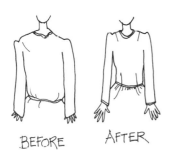

BEFORE   AFTER

Fig. 5–4

If the garment is too big, take it in. Sometimes you can restitch the seams so that the entire garment is narrower. You may have to take it in on several seams or create new darts, so that the fitting (particularly in the bodice) moves to the correct location as well. Rarely, you can gather across the shoulders and take it in at the waist, and be fine. The bodice will become very loose and blousy. It depends upon the era and how unfashionable you may be with this particular treatment.

For Victorian dresses, you can usually remove the waistband and regather the skirt to narrow the waist without losing the volume of the garment. And during eras when there were oversleeves and undersleeves, adjustments are simple. The undersleeve doesn't show very much, and the oversleeve was big anyway.

To make a man's garment smaller, plan to take it in a bit on all vertical seams. The simpler cut of men's clothing makes it essential to keep the seams at the correct position on the body. Some bodices, such as a man's vest, will need to be taken in at the waist and the shoulders to achieve a successful fit.

A too-long garment usually needs simple hemming. However, if you have a ruffle or furbelow (showy trimming), you may need to shorten the garment directly above this trim. In some cases, you'll also need to gather or take in the trim a bit, as well.

You'll have to decide the context of your character. Perhaps you're trying to alter a second-hand garment that was made for a larger woman. In thinking about this, you might decide that it was a garment that your character received as a "hand-me-down" from a large-bodied relative. In that context, you don't have to struggle to make it look as if it were originally made for your character.

Letting Out

If you're enlarging a second-hand garment, you may want to pick through "rag bags" in antique and used clothing shops, to find

Fig. 5–5

GUSSET

Fig. 5–6

scraps of fabric that match the color and era of your garment. You'll use these scraps to make inserts, gussets, or panels to enlarge the garment.

Often, you can rip out gathering and ease it into a larger size. This is particularly easy with the fuller Victorian clothes. For a new, larger waistband, I recommend matching a contemporary velvet to your Victorian garment. If the waistband is going to be snug anyway, the fabric had better be new in order to withstand the strain. As a general rule, avoid actual, old fabric in areas where the fabric will be under stress.

Adding Gussets and Panels

To enlarge tight sleeves or shoulders, you can conceal a gusset under the arm. Try to match the fabric as closely as possible, so the gusset won't be too noticeable. Open the seams that meet under the arm, and see how much fabric needs to be added (Fig. 5–5). Cut a diamond-shaped gusset to fit, including a seam allowance. Baste this in, and adjust as necessary before doing your final stitching.

Women's clothing is easier than men's clothing to alter, but men's fashions often had gussets to start with, which are an asset when re-fitting a garment.

A gusset at the back center seam will enlarge men's trousers accurately. Open the center back seam, cut a triangular piece of matching fabric to enlarge the fit of the trousers as necessary, and baste it in place (Fig. 5–6). Adjust as necessary and do your final stitching. If your gentleman tends to gain and lose inches frequently, cut the gusset to make the trousers as large as they might possibly be needed. Before finally sewing in the gusset, make two short straps of the same fabric, one with a buckle on the end. This will be stitched in place to adjust to his current size (Fig. 5–7). This will work on vests, too, making them somewhat adjustable.

A man's vest may need such a large gusset or panel in the back that he'll have to keep his coat on to conceal the alteration. Of course, if he's wearing a tight-fitting frock coat, he'll probably want to leave it on, anyway: It's too difficult to get in and out of a frock coat to do so frequently.

Gussets also appeared in women's clothing, though not as frequently. If you need to add a large gusset or panel to a woman's Victorian gown or skirt, it is often wise to use a contrasting fabric

Fig. 5–7

to make the addition look planned. Velvet looks nice against silk, and vice versa.

Making Invisible Alterations

Use trim to conceal where a Victorian garment was altered. Braid can be placed at the waist, or over newly altered seams. A contrasting ruffle can lengthen a skirt where the hem is too narrow, or where the original fabric faded so the hem material is too dark.

Whatever alteration is necessary, use materials that look correct and stick close to the mode of the era. Then, no matter what alterations you do, they can be explained in the context of history. Clothes were rarely discarded when they didn't fit: They were altered, restyled as fashions changed, and worn until they wore out.

If you can find fabric that is from the era of the garment you're altering, be certain that it is strong enough, particularly if it will be under stress. Otherwise, work with modern fabrics that look like the older materials.

If discreet alterations are impossible, be outrageous instead. The dandies of past eras wore clothing that would stop traffic. Plan to do the same with your fashions. Add a series of ruffles to cover an incongruous addition or a seam that didn't alter well, if ruffles were correct in your era. Find a stunning shawl that will draw attention away from the fitting errors in your gown. Give him an opulent, overdone vest to keep friends from noticing the gusset that doesn't match his frock coat. Above all, the costume should be worn as if it is the most marvelous outfit ever invented. If you wear a garment as if it fit perfectly, no one will notice that it doesn't. If you're constantly tugging at your clothing, you'll lose the battle. People will look at it more critically to see why you need to continually adjust it.

When all else fails, trade your costume with someone who *can* wear it. Perhaps he or she has something hidden in the closet that will fit you.

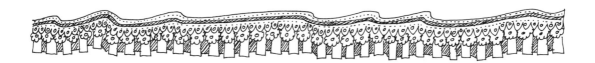

CHAPTER 6

How to Buy Reproductions

I f you don't sew, you'll be interested in two kinds of historical clothes: those that are custom made for you, and those that are off-the-rack, truly ready-to-wear.

COMMISSIONING CUSTOM CLOTHING

You can order custom-made clothing through a mail order company that specializes in historical clothing. Many ready-to-wear historical costumers make custom clothing, too (see Resources listing). One of them might be in your area, which makes fitting extra easy, but not essential.

You may prefer to deal with a seamstress or tailor in your neighborhood. Start with the Yellow Pages, under Tailoring; Clothing, Custom Made; Wedding Apparel, and similar headings. Dry cleaners often have a tailor working on the premises. Call to ask if they have experience with historical costuming. (Professionals often hate the word "costume," and prefer to use the term "historical clothing.") Another way to locate someone who sews cos-

Janet Burgess and Milan A Vodick, active participants in Civil War reenactments, are shown wearing reproductions of the era, typical of readymade clothing available from Amazon. Photo courtesy of Amazon Dry Goods.

HERE!

Fig. 6–1

tumes is to check with local living history groups, theaters, and fabric stores.

You will want someone who agrees with you on the degree of historical accuracy necessary. Clothing that one person sees as "close enough" to accurate may be an outrage to a purist. Or you may be handed a shocking bill when the seamstress (or tailor—I'm going to use the terms alternately, to avoid sexism here) spent more time and money for accuracy that you really needed.

Materials

You should agree upon all-natural fabrics, blends, or synthetics, depending upon your purpose for the clothing. A one-time costume may be fine in a budget-priced synthetic, but review the section on synthetics, in Chapter 3. An *accurate* costume starts with natural fibers.

Talk about your budget. If you can afford a handwoven, perfectly accurate fabric, you'll be disappointed if your seamstress buys regular dressweight cotton at the discount fabric shop. Clearly state the color, weight, weave, and price of the fabric, as accurately as you can. Better yet, go to the shop together to select the fabric and notions. Read Chapter 3 about selecting colors. Don't waste money on fabric that will make you look like an overgrown turnip, or a celery stalk gone awry!

If you want hooks-and-eyes in a location where the tailor is accustomed to placing a zipper, be certain that he knows what you want. Otherwise, he is going to feel justified in using his regular, contemporary construction techniques.

For costume-party wear, you might be able to adapt a second-hand contemporary garment, as described in the chapter on short-cuts. Explore this idea with your seamstress or tailor, if you want to economize.

Design

If you need an accurate design, be certain that your seamstress knows this. Some commercial patterns may look "just like" what you want, to your seamstress. See what pattern she is using, and what modifications are being made. Be certain that it is exactly what you want, before she cuts the fabric. Get an exact sketch of the completed garment. If she says "We're going to make the sleeves fuller here," have her draw exactly what the finished

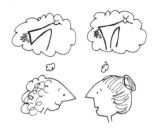

Fig. 6–2

sleeves will look like. If the finished garment isn't what you thought she was describing, you can *see* where things went wrong, if you have a sketch that you've both agreed upon.

If you are adapting a contemporary dress pattern, an important point is the width of the skirt. A too-narrow skirt can ruin a Civil War era gown, while a daydress from the 1880s can be spoiled by a skirt that isn't narrow enough. If you have an illustration of the gown that you want to copy, a simple technique will guarantee that your skirt will look like the one in the picture. This technique is the "Amazon Theory of Hoop Relativity," and you'll find it described in *Clothing Guidelines for the Civil War Era* by Janet Burgess (see References). Basically, you're comparing the width of the skirt to the height of the woman wearing it, but a simple doubling of the hem width in the illustration will not give you a proportionately accurate skirt; skirts are *round*, so you need a circumference measurement. Well, if you're a math whiz, you can figure this yourself. If you're like me (a math teacher's nightmare), I recommend using Janet's Amazon Theory.

Sewing Techniques

Before you commission a garment, discuss how much historically accurate handsewing will go into it. Handsewing can be the most expensive part. If the stitches won't show anyway, consider machine stitching for strength and economy. The seams won't look as soft as with handsewing, but the garment will be far more affordable. Some of the companies listed in the Resources section will make entirely handsewn garments.

Unless your garment represents an era after the invention of sewing machines, do not allow your tailor to topstitch or hem with a sewing machine. No machine stitches should show on the outside of the garment. This includes buttonholes.

Delivery Date

If you need the garment for a party or event, be certain your seamstress knows this. As you know by now, it is easy to get caught up in historical costuming. In pursuit of perfection, your seamstress may not realize that this project is taking too long for your purpose. As you approach the deadline, check with her in case she has questions or problems that might delay the work.

Accessorizing

What do you do while you're waiting for your custom-made gown to be completed? Locate accessories. Accessories can make or break an outfit.

For pre-Civil War accessories, your best bet is to locate reproductions. Several excellent mail-order sources are listed under Resources. With the correct hat and shoes, and a purse or pocket filled with historically accurate goodies, you'll feel terrific and dazzle your friends.

Puffed ball gown of the Civil War Era, designed, made and modeled by Heidi Marsh. Photo courtesy of Heidi Marsh.

Cordovan wrap gown, designed, made and modeled by Heidi Marsh. Photo courtesy of Heidi Marsh.

For more contemporary accessories, you may find what you need in local antique and vintage clothing shops. You should call ahead to see if they carry items from "your" era, but don't expect an accurate answer. Many shops are so cluttered that even the owners don't know what they have. Also, you can often adapt an accessory from another era to suit your needs.

BEFORE AFTER

Fig. 6–3

In 1985, I needed an 1890s straw hat. I found some nice, pricey reproductions, and a few authentic hats that were out of my budget as well. However, in one of my favorite, cluttered secondhand clothing shops, I located a 1940s (or 50s?) hat covered with shredded net and sadly crushed fake fruit. I paid $4 for it, and in my car I tore off the trim. As I suspected, the hat had been "built" on a perfect, old, 1890s straw hat (Fig. 6–3). The manufacturer probably bought the old hats at an auction or found them in his back room, and added mountains of decoration to disguise them.

Be certain to read Chapter 7, Buying Wearables, before you visit antique and vintage clothing shops. You may avoid an expensive mistake.

SELECTING READYMADE REPRODUCTIONS

Ordering by Mail

Fig. 6–4

If you choose readymade reproductions, there are a number of considerations. First, you may be disappointed in the quality of sewing from a mail-order source. In some cases, you *should* be — it is a good sign. Even with a sewing machine, middle-class women didn't have much time for sewing. Many garments were hastily thrown together and they looked it! So don't expect sewing that compares with what you see in today's readymade garments, if the historical garment represents the middle class or is inexpensive. A company does not know what your purpose is when you place an order. Some companies specialize in affordable costumes that are "close enough" to suit a casual approach to history. Price is not always a guideline to accuracy; I know one source of magnificent Victorian and Edwardian clothing, and I have no idea how their garments are so low in price. However, other companies have low prices because their clothing looks okay for the era if you don't examine it too closely. Their garments are fully machine stitched so

Fig. 6–5

they will go through the washer and dryer without a problem. But you'll wince if you order this clothing for a living history project.

To avoid the *bad* kind of disappointment, check with the company to see if machine stitching will show on the outside of a pre-1870s garment. This includes hems, collars, buttonholes, and eyelets. On a Colonial mob cap or Regency bonnet, you'll be disappointed if the brim is hemmed or reinforced with machine stitching and you need something historically perfect. In other cases, you won't care because it is only for a costume party. But ask these questions ahead of time if the information isn't in the catalogue. In some cases, the catalogue descriptions will make this question unnecessary, so read closely before asking.

Some excellent seamstresses of the nineteenth century could make such even, tiny stitches that the sewing looks as if it were done on a sewing machine. Only close inspection will reveal the slight differences. This is not an excuse to wear clothing with inaccurate machine stitching that shows, but a point of interest.

Check with several companies before ordering. In fact, I recommend ordering every catalogue available for your era. You'll find a wide range of prices. There are several reasons why an item may be far less expensive from one source than from another. A company may deal in enough volume to sustain low prices and still make a profit. Another may have found a manufacturer going out of business (there just isn't the market for hatpins that there used to be. . .), and bought the goods at a ridiculously low price, passing the economy along to customers as long as the supply lasts. Or, a concern may be selling actual antiques that aren't as usable as reproductions. For example, the metal in antique hatpins is often brittle and will snap easily. If you're trying to weave a pin through a mountain of hair and an impenetrable hat, the pin may break the first time you use it. I've had this happen several times. Now I use reproduction hatpins whenever possible.

Another reason for price differences is how valuable the owner considers his or her time. A woman who makes and sells Medieval patterns as a hobby can afford to charge less for them than a woman who is supporting her family with her pattern-making business. A nonprofit organization that is supported by state or federal funds can charge far less for its items than a company that must at least break even.

A final reason why one item may be much lower in price than another is poor quality. An ivory-look plastic fan will certainly cost less than a real ivory one. However, a flimsy, imported tricorn may have the same description ("black felt tricorn with gold braid trim") as a nice, heavy quality tricorn. So check the return policy, and deal with firms whose merchandise you've liked in the past. The list of mail-order catalogues in the Resources section includes budget lines as well as high-quality firms. To some of you, the budget companies will be "cheap, not worth trying," while others will think that the higher quality folks are overcharging for merchandise that is much too fancy. For this reason, read lots of catalogues and compare. A small first order is recommended until you see how well you like a company's merchandise and service. Most companies are very good about accepting return merchandise, as long as it is still in "brand new" condition. However, don't plan to wear the item once for a costume party, and then return it. That's not fair to the dealer and it's not fair to the rest of us. If enough people do this, the dealer is likely to change his or her return policy. When you're accustomed to dealing with brand new items, it's easy to tell when something has been worn.

When dealing with mail-order sources of historical clothing and accessories, keep in mind that a business may not be profitable enough for the owner to quit his or her daytime job. Thus, after working at a 9-to-5 job, a person goes home to face a mountain of orders. Some people can afford clerical help, but most cannot. Many are in business to help others find items for their favorite era. They are doing this as a service, not as a moneymaker. Therefore, at times, catalogues and merchandise may be slow in arriving. If you absolutely *must* have an item by a certain date or it is worthless to you, please state this clearly when you order.

The majority of companies in this specialty give excellent service, so I don't want to scare you away from ordering. However, delays can happen. Some customers may not understand how a person can put personal priorities ahead of business (especially when it involves *their* money), but it is a fact of life in cottage industries. All it takes are a few angry, antagonistic letters, and the person quits. And that's one less source of the historical items we need. So keep your inquiries pleasant.

Over many years of dealing with small and large historical clothing companies, I have *never* heard of anyone cheating a customer. If your order is late, check on it right away in case it was lost in transit. And in the case of readymade items, cancel the order if it is not going to arrive when you need it. Order it from another source. (Another good reason to have several catalogues on hand.)

Here's another tip: When you hear about a new source of an item that you want, contact the source right away. It may take years for the business to produce the item, and you'll want to be near the top of the waiting list. Recently, a noble soul has been trying to work with a manufacturer to produce high-top boots and shoes with button fastenings. She has worked on prototypes with several possible manufacturers, and at last report she was optimistic about production starting soon. Many of us have been following her endeavors closely, hoping that she will be successful. This is the way that many historically accurate items become available, but I expect that she'll spend her first year filling orders from her waiting list.

Planning Your Historical Wardrobe

Select your readymade historical clothing the same way that you buy your everyday wardrobe. Choose colors and styles that work well together; see sample wardrobe, Fig. 6–6. If you're interested in several eras, try to find items that are easy to adapt from one time period to another. Particularly for the Victorian years, you can devote a whole, oversized closet to your gowns if you don't plan carefully.

An item that was worn in earlier years may be fine for later years. However, you cannot wear a more contemporary garment for an earlier time period. A man's 1890s sack suit may be fine for 1920, but *not* appropriate for 1860. This may sound perfectly obvious, but it is amazing how many people forget it. Take advantage of earlier, adaptable fashions if you can. For example, my 1860s daydress can be worn with a more extreme bustle and an overskirt, and a cape over the shoulders, to look like an early 1890s outfit. Your early Medieval gown may adapt to later years with an overtunic, jewelry, and more elaborate veiling. Fashions seem to go in cycles, and you can use this to keep your historical wardrobe small, versatile, and affordable.

SEWING AND COLLECTING VINTAGE FASHIONS

bonnet

hat

lace-up boots

shoes or slippers

black wool cape

white cotton blouse

white 1890's blouse

black silk blouse

camisole or corset cover

corset

drawers

black skirt in wool or silk

white cotton skirt

petticoats

hoop skirt or bustle

overskirt

An adaptable Victorian wardrobe

Fig. 6-6

CHAPTER 7
Buying Wearables

Some people believe that no garment from the past should be worn for any reason, because it will be destroyed with wear and we'll lose that piece of history. I agree with those concerned with preserving history. But I can also understand the view that clothing should not be locked up in someone's climate-controlled closet where it is never seen, and *still* deteriorates (albeit more slowly). I think that any garment that is in near-perfect condition or has historic significance should be in a museum where it will be displayed for people to study and enjoy. Everything else should be enjoyed by its owner according to his or her own dictates. If clothing remains in a dark closet as part of a cherished collection, that is fine. If the owner wears the pieces every day and gets immense pleasure from them, then that is an option as well.

So, with that basic philosophy in mind, let's talk about wearables. Wearables are old or antique clothing that can be worn. They are historical clothing, but we call them wearables because they are neither rare nor perfect. These clothes may need repairs, or may have been hastily made when new. Above all, they are fun bits of history to include with your historical or contemporary clothing.

Wearables from the 1950s; dress and hat from display at the 1987 Tampa Vintage Clothing Show.

WHERE TO FIND WEARABLES

Auctions

Auctions are great sources of wearables. There are auctions of vintage and antique clothing, and sometimes they have great buys. The ratty clothes that need repair will go for a song, while shopowners pay dearly for pieces that can go on the rack immediately.

Fig. 7–1

There are also household auctions, which are often equally likely sources. In a box with chipped china and toy trucks that were missing wheels, I've found perfect lace collars. In a hopeless wad of 1950s housedresses, I found a repairable parasol that is now one of my treasures. The only problem with household auctions is that you are competing with shopowners who may want other items in the box or lot. Or with a shopowner who knows the value of the clothing. And an occasional competing bidder will know what you're interested in, and bid against you because he thinks it must be worth at least as much as you're willing to pay.

Often you will find auctions listed in the Sunday newspapers; you'll also see auction houses listed in the Yellow Pages, and you can call them to find out when they have auctions containing textiles or clothing. Some antique dealers will also tell you about auctions, especially if they do not deal in clothing. Those who do carry clothing aren't likely to tell you where they are buying their merchandise; the dealer wants you to be her customer instead.

Look bored, no matter what

Fig. 7–2

Here are a few tips when you go to an auction: First of all, examine the merchandise carefully. Do not be afraid to take items out of boxes, hold them up to the light, and study them closely. However, you should look thoroughly bored, and finally shake your head as if you're disappointed. Auctions are a game, and you never want to look too interested in any item. A dealer who knows very little about textiles will take your cue and bid against you, if you look too excited over something.

At the preview before the auction, pay attention to who else is studying the clothing carefully. Also, if items are in "box lots" (containers filled with an assortment of items), you'll want to see who is studying other items in the box besides the clothing. If you later find yourself bidding against a very determined man, it will help to know that he ignored the clothing and really wants the toy trucks. You may be able to make a deal with him later.

At the preview, you should also make notes to yourself about the item number and how high you'll bid for it. You might want to make notes about the items in each box, in case you forget during the bidding. In addition if you set a spending limit for each item, it can save you an expensive mistake. It's easy to get caught up in enthusiastic bidding and find yourself spending far more than the value of the item, just to be the "winner."

There is a certain strategy to where you sit. Sometimes the auctioneer will take the bid from the person sitting nearest him (that is, at the front) if there are several bidders offering the same price. Or, if you're in a crowd where the auctioneer is easily distracted, he may never see or hear your bid from the back of the hall. In fact, many dealers put marks on the front row seats, to reserve them. Another reason for sitting in front is to see the items displayed by the runners (people who carry the items and hold them up for view during the bidding). Sometimes, I have overlooked an item in a box and needed to see it more closely when the bidding began. From the front, I could see it well enough to guess the value.

A final reason to choose a front-row seat is to be certain that the item you want is still in the box. Unscrupulous bidders sometimes move items from box to box, right before bidding starts, hoping to fool competitors. Such unsavory types usually place a valuable item in another box filled with junk. A real sneak will do his best to conceal the item, packing a beaded lace collar into a broken vacuum cleaner. Auction houses watch for this sort of thing, but they can't keep an eye on everyone. If you see someone moving items from box to box, alert the management. They want bidding to be fair. Their reputation depends upon it. Be certain that *your* item is still in the box when the bidding starts. If you ask about an item you can't see from the back, you're telling the rest of the bidders that this is something of interest. The price will start climbing, particularly if the audience thinks you're a pro.

Conversely, there are reasons for staying near the back of the hall during bidding. From the front seat, you'll rarely see your competitors. It isn't possible to scan the entire crowd in back of you and keep bidding, too. If you stand at the back of the hall, you can see your competitor; if he is the high bidder, approach him later for the item you wanted. But don't count on it. Generally, auction-goers are part of a network. If the new box-owner thinks that an item in the box is valuable, he'll often wait to see if he can get more for it elsewhere. Of course, if you are the successful bidder, you can offer to sell him the items he's interested in. Never bid more for a box lot than you would pay for the item or items you want. If you aren't a pro, it's risky to bid higher, planning to recover the excess by selling items you don't want.

Another advantage to a back-row seat is that you can guess how close you are to being the successful bidder. You can see if your competitors are raising their hands or cards slowly because they're nearing their spending limit. It's a shame to miss out on an item when you could have had it for just $2 more. But don't keep bidding past your established limit. If the other bidder gets the item and you cannot live without it, you can always get his name and phone number, and offer to buy the item at a profit.

You are the only one who can decide the best seating strategy, and it will vary from auction to auction. If the runners aren't going to display many items in the box, you might as well sit at the back. If you didn't get time to examine each lot carefully, then sit in front.

Another strategy is to take a smart bidder with you. I've met several women who have very astute daughters. At auctions and yard sales, my younger daughter has either an "eagle eye" or the most remarkable intuition. When she tells me to bid at an auction, or to stop at a particular yard sale, I always do: She has led me to some tremendous bargains. She also has her own collection of beaded bags, bought at auctions with birthday money. Some of her best buys were when she was five years old. If you have a similar helpmate, take him or her with you, especially if you gamble on sitting in the back of the auction hall.

Remember that dealers will usually bid up to half the retail value of the item. Once in a while, if a dealer is certain he can resell the item, he will go higher than half retail. The only people who will bid in the range of the actual retail value of an item are collectors such as you and me. And some collectors will bid much higher than the retail value, if they need that specific item for their collections. However, do not assume that all dealers are bidding half the retail value of the item. Some may be buying for their own collections, not for resale. Many collectors became dealers because they had so many extra items from their box lots that it became worthwhile to go into business.

I once bid for a Victorian bonnet and watched the price exceed twice what it would have cost in a shop. After the auction, I asked the couple why they paid so much for the bonnet. It turned out to be a style that they needed to complete their collection, and they were prepared to bid even higher. They invited me to their shop, because they had similar bonnets at much lower prices. The ones in the shop weren't quite right for their collection, but suited me just fine.

At both yard sales and auctions, you'll discover that there are "regulars." They may or may not be your competitors when you're buying wearables. It pays to know exactly what their interests are. For example, if you are buying clothes and another person is buying quilts, you may sit together at auctions and decide ahead of time how you'll divide a box lot that has both items in it.

If you know who collects buttons, you may be able to buy from them at the end of the auction. Button collectors often strip the buttons right off the clothing. And the clothing ends up in the dumpster, or in a box they'll sell at a flea market, just to get rid of it.

Share information with these people — that's called networking. If you saw some great quilts at a yard sale, tell the quilt collector when you see her at a later yard sale. Who knows? The button collector you helped once may steer you toward a box of clothes at an auction that are only missing buttons.

If you aren't certain of the value of an item, just bid what it is worth to you. You may decide to go over the retail value, to save the bother of locating a similar item. It can be worth an extra $10 if you save three hours of driving from shop to shop.

Yard Sales

Another great source of wearables. Use logic when you plan your yard sale-ing routes. Visit the neighborhoods with the oldest residents, and also those with the best likelihood of having junk-packed attics and basements. In New England, I used the newspapers to locate promising-sounding yard sales. On Friday nights, I studied a map and planned my route to visit the most yard sales at the earliest hour possible. In the part of Florida where I live now, most yard sales are not advertised, so I have a regular route that I follow, looking for signs.

Fig. 7-3

Neighborhoods with older retired people are worthwhile. The children of these people are often running the yard sales. They don't have any sentimental attachment to the Victorian cape that needs mending. They don't need the best price for the items, because they're just cleaning out the basement for Mom or Dad.

The tackiest yard sales can have the most affordable treasures. In 1987, I bought handpainted 1940s ties at a yard sale for five cents each. And they were in perfect condition, on a coat hanger in back of the shiny, polyester housedresses. Now they're part of my husband's wardrobe. It pays to look thoroughly.

You can usually size up a yard sale by checking the prices on the first four or five items you see. Some people go to second-hand merchandise stores to check prices. Then they mark their goods accordingly: This is the yard sale where you cannot talk the owner down from $15 for a patched pair of Victorian drawers, because "that's $5 less than what the stores charge for them." Walk away from a sale like this. It is hopeless to point out that these drawers aren't nearly as good as the $20 ones in the shops. Don't argue with the person or make offers that she will take as an insult. Be cheerful and go back to the sale at the end of the day when the owner will be ready to bargain. (If you've been insulting to her earlier, she'll throw the stuff away before selling it to you.)

At yard sales and flea markets, I never offer anyone less than half their asking price. In some cases, any offer less than the asking price is going to be offensive; listen to how other offers are being received before making yours. Whatever you do, don't get the seller annoyed, or you won't be able to bargain the price down at the end of the day.

Flea Markets

Flea markets are not as reliable as yard sales. If it is a flea market where most of the tables are owned by dealers, bargains are rare. However, I have bought wonderful clothes from dealers who sold entirely different goods. Some of them bought boxes of goods at auctions, just to get the china or jewelry: They could care less about the 1890s parasol that needs repair. If you're the first one to spot it in the pile that says "Anything here for 50 cents," you're in luck. This dealer is also likely to give you a special price if you'll take several bulky clothing items off his hands.

At a real flea market with many tables rented by people who are cleaning out their attics, you may find some treasures. Get there when the tables are being set up, because the dealers are there too, trying to grab the best items first.

Rummage Sales

Rarely great sources of wearables, rummage sales should be well down on your list. The women who set these up usually take the best items home. With the popularity of vintage clothing among celebrities, many moms will seize the best old-fashioned garb for their daughters. However, now and then rummage sales are set up by people who don't know the value of vintage wear, or just don't care. Again, you're competing with dealers, so wait in line before the doors open, and *run* to scan the clothing as soon as you get in.

Second-Hand Clothing Shops

Thrift stores and Goodwill shops are regularly picked over by dealers and fashionably dressed students. Still, an occasional treasure escapes their notice. Find out when new merchandise will be put on display, and get there as early as you can.

Vintage Clothing Shops

Nearly everyone of these stores will have a "bargain rack," with clothes that haven't sold and/or need repair. When the shopowners buy a box of items at an auction, this is the rack where they put the clothes that they regard as fairly worthless. One woman's trash is another woman's treasure.

Antique Shops

At the bottom of my list for finding good buys in wearables are general antique shops. Condition is often more important than age, so an antique dealer is likely to display only garments in really excellent condition. And the price is often set by the person who sold it to the dealer. (You know, the salesman says, "Hey, you can get $200 for this one, e-a-s-y!" One has to wonder why the salesman didn't sell it at retail himself, if it was so easy.)

On the other hand, if a dealer took a chance on some Victorian gowns, and they've been in the store for awhile, you may be in luck. Clothing takes up a lot of space. At some point, the dealer is likely to take any price for the clothing, just to gain space for items with a better profit margin and quicker turnover.

To locate shops that carry old clothing, you'll need to check several headings in the Yellow Pages. Among the most common headings are: Antiques; Apparel, Used; Clothing, Used; Consignment Shops, Used Clothing; Second-Hand Shops; Thrift Shops; and Women's Apparel, Used.

PURCHASING GUIDELINES

Most auctions, yard sales, and flea markets want payment in cash only. Plan accordingly, and take more than you think you'll spend. It can be heartbreaking to leave a magnificent, affordable item because you didn't bring enough cash. Some rummage sales and second-hand shops will take checks, but don't count on it. Most antique dealers will take personal checks only if you have a mountain of identification, such as credit cards.

No matter where you buy your wearables, be a smart shopper. There are a number of questions to answer before you buy.

How old is it?

First of all, you aren't likely to find anything older than the nineteenth century in wearable condition. I have had people try to sell me "Colonial" garments made by machine, so beware! The women who told me these tales were quite sincere, and I'm certain that it was a misunderstanding passed down from an older relative. Most shopowners who deal in textiles have a reputation to maintain and will try to accurately represent each piece in their shop. But now and then you'll find someone who personally manufactures the histories of his or her merchandise.

The sewing machine wasn't patented until 1846 and was not in general use until 1865. However, older garments were sometimes reinforced or altered with a sewing machine. And the better seamstresses of the nineteenth century could sew such perfect, even stitches that it is difficult to tell their work from machine stitching.

Historical romance authors in costumes appropriate to their novels. From left, Janelle Taylor, Kathryn Falk, and Elaine Barbieri. Photo courtesy of Romantic Times Publishing Group.

I'm telling you this so that you won't pay extra for a wearable that someone represents as being very, very old There are more details related to dating textiles in Chapter 8. In this chapter, we're assuming that most wearable vintage and antique garments are from the years after the Civil War.

Can you really wear it?

During the nineteenth century, certain fabric treatments that aren't practiced today weakened fibers. Some fabrics were made heavier with powders, much as we use sizing; unfortunately, they dried out some fabrics. Other fabrics were treated with dyes that dried the fibers or actually ate through them. The darker colors such as purple, blue, and brown, are most noted for this problem. Finally, it is the nature of some fabrics to wear out. Some get threadbare, and others just lose their resilience. This is the biggest problem when buying wearables: The fabric that "just has a little tear" is the fabric that may be in shreds in a week. Silk is notorious for this.

The rule is this: If the tear is on a seam, you might be able to repair it. You'll then have a wonderful wearable garment that you'll enjoy for years. If the tear is not on a seam, there is a good possibility that it is the first of many tears that will appear in a short period of time. In some cases, these garments were in museum collections, stored in climate-controlled rooms. The museums sold the clothes because they really weren't so valuable and the museum needed the space. Then the garments sat in a dusty auction house, where age quickly caught up with them. (Remember the movie *Lost Horizon*, where the woman aged suddenly when she left that youth-preserving realm? Same effect.)

When checking fabric for the likelihood of future tears, hold it up to the light and look through it as best you can. You will be able to see if there are weak areas. Especially check the elbows on blouses and the back panels of skirts. These are the areas that have already had wear, and the tears are likely to appear there first.

If the fabric looks strong enough, you'll want to study its texture. Check how dry the fabric seems. Examine it closely for dust in the crevices. Dust can dry a fabric and cause it to age very quickly.

How faded is it? This will affect the texture of the fibers and result in premature aging. A fabric that looks brown or brownish-purple is often the sign of one of those fiber-weakening dyes. Check for holes that look like moths have been munching. They are usually the first areas where the dyes have eaten through the fabric. Don't buy it.

However, if the fabric still looks fine, crunch a small area in your hand. I'm *not* telling you to damage the fabric or wrinkle it horribly. You are only going to compress it enough to see if it springs back to its original shape easily. Don't confuse this with how easily it wrinkles. Even linen that was made yesterday wrinkles easily.

Using light to detect wear

Fig. 7-4

It will tear here.

Can you disguise the damage?

Check the seams to see if the fabric is weaker along the stitching. You may have to hold it up to the light again for this. If the garment's former owner was a "chub" and was straining the seams, you may have a lot of reinforcing to do, to make the item wearable. If fabric around the seams is already weakened from strain, you may have to take the garment in an inch or two to have a sturdy seam. Be certain that you can still wear it if it must be taken in that much.

See what repair work must be done, and what you can do to disguise it. I had a 1940s gown that was torn and had a burn on the upper bodice. I sold it to a dealer who then put wonderful, gaudy sequined patches over the damaged areas. These panels extended over the shoulders; it looked as if the gown were originally made that way.

Stain covered by fabric flowers

Fig. 7–5

If you fall in love with a garment that is ready to shred, you might want to create a lining for it. The lining would be the same color as the garment, but smaller. With this lining in place, you can get some wear from the garment and not put so much stress on the weakened fabric. This will buy you just a little time, because the fabric is going to shred even if it just hangs in the closet.

Lace and tucks can be used to cover damage on a Victorian garment, if you're absolutely certain that the existing damage isn't the harbinger of worse decay. Try to use fabric treatments (we're talking fabric art here, not chemicals and such) that look correct for the period. Bargain-basement nylon lace will never look right on a Civil War ball gown.

Fig. 7–6

Victorian undergarments are often damaged. Frankly, I'd be intimidated by a perfect pair of drawers but I cheerfully wear a pair that has numerous patches by former owners. And sometimes you can have fun with the patches, if you're going to wear the undergarments where they will be seen. I like to keep my patches of the same white percale as the garment. However, embroidering the edges of the patch can be a nice touch (Fig. 7–6). My favorite is a nice white embroidery thread for this. It is subtle, but amusing. A feather stitch and some french knots can add texture to the patch, and make the garment more interesting. On other undergarments, patches alone are enough. For example, a lace-decked petticoat would look overdone with any more decoration. Stark white patches are a nice contrast, and don't detract from the beauty of the original garment.

How much should you pay?

If you've examined the garment and know that it is overpriced, but you want it anyway, sometimes you can haggle with the shopowner. The appropriate way to ask is, "Would you consider a lower price for this?" Many shopowners will give you a blunt, "No," and that is that. Others may be novices in old clothing, and you can point out why the price should be lower. Sometimes, even experienced dealers make mistakes.

Recently, I asked a dealer if she would take a lower price for a hoop skirt I needed. It was a contemporary reproduction, with plastic hoops and an elastic waistband. At first, the dealer said "No" quite firmly. As soon as she saw me getting ready to leave, she added that she'd seen similar hoopskirts at flea markets, for double and triple her asking price. I agreed with her, adding that those were undoubtedly actual antiques. Once I showed her why the hoopskirt was a reproduction, she happily sold it to me at half the price she'd asked first. But at no time did I try to argue with her, tell her that she was "wrong," or whine about the price. It was just one intelligent woman pointing out an easily made error to another intelligent woman.

This is an important point. Even the most experienced dealer or collector can be uncertain about specific eras or items. Please don't deliberately try to upset a shopowner to get the price lower; that is the sort of thing that makes shopping difficult for the rest of us. However, if you are certain of the facts, you may be doing the shopowner a favor by explaining an error. The woman who sold me the hoopskirt would still have it at its inflated price, if I hadn't pointed out the error.

CARING FOR FRAGILE WEARABLES

Cleaning and Laundering

Keep wearables as clean as possible to preserve them longer. Ask local textile collectors and galleries for the name of the best dry cleaner. Before you trust your clothing to that cleaner, talk with the manager and be certain that he or she knows how to handle valuable old clothing.

If your clothing is safe to launder, be certain to use a soap that will wash out entirely. I wash few vintage items in the machine, but when I do, I use Shaklee's Basic L. All other detergents I've used leave a residue that I can feel and/or smell. These perfume-y residues will contribute to the decay of the fabric. Most products sold especially for "gentle" washing seem to have a perfume that remains in the fabric. This can dry out the fibers. Avoid them.

For hand washables, I use Shaklee's Basic H in a very dilute solution of about ¼ teaspoon of Basic H to a quart of water. I also rinse my clothing thoroughly, to be extra certain that all soapy residues are removed. I never use soaps or detergents sold for washing sweaters and hand washables. All of these seem to leave perfumed residues, as do most liquid soaps sold for washing dishes.

To locate Shaklee products, check your Yellow Pages. They are most often listed under Cleaning Products, Retail; Nutritional Products; Vitamins; or Health Foods.

A wet garment is often weakened by the water. In addition, there can be more strain on the fibers and seams, if the garment is heavier from the absorbed water. If the garment is very delicate, here is my trick to lift it out of the sink or tub without damage:

1. Put a clean pillowcase (or other strong, white piece of fabric) in the water while the sink is still full. It should be underneath the garment, and as flat as possible, so that you won't have to rearrange the garment later.

2. Let the water drain out of the sink or tub. Then you may want to carefully arrange the wet garment on the pillowcase so that it is as flat as possible. At this point, you may want to blot the garment with a clean, white towel, to remove excess water. Of course, you'll be pressing wrinkles into the garment when you do this, which will necessitate extra (heat-damaging) ironing later. If possible, leave the garment undisturbed once it has been arranged on the pillowcase.

3. Carefully lift the pillowcase so that the garment is evenly supported. You may need help with this if the garment is large and/or heavy.

4. Arrange so that it is flat as it dries. There are elevated screens sold for drying sweaters, and these work well for small items. For larger items, I've heard of people using clean, framed porch screens. The screen must be supported so that air circulates

through the garment easily. If the pillowcase prevents air circulation, be very careful in lifting the garment off the pillowcase to place it on the screen. With someone else to help you, you might be able to place your drying screen on top of the garment, and then turn the whole sandwich over so that the pillowcase is on top. Then merely lift it off.

5. Be certain to keep the garment out of direct sun while it dries. Be equally certain that it dries quickly, to prevent mildew. In humid climates, judicious use of a hand-held hairdryer may be advisable. Use a cool or warm setting for the hairdryer, and move it constantly to prevent heat buildup.

Stain Removal

Stains require special treatment. First of all, use the gentlest cleaner that is likely to work. I once ruined a blouse with a series of gentle but fiber-weakening treatments that weren't strong enough to remove rust. One application of Zud (a rust-removing cleaner sold at grocery stores) would have solved the problem. On the other hand, I've used cleaners with bleach, and found that the fabric was too weak to stand up to it. Each of these accidents was heartbreaking.

The safest rule is never to buy a garment with a stain that prevents its wear. Of course, if you're a gambler like me, you'll take chances on stained clothing, and sometimes you'll be thrilled when the stain washes right out. More often you'll be disappointed, but the victories make it all worthwhile. And permanently stained clothing can often be remodeled into something wearable, or used to repair another garment.

Assuming that you're going to gamble, here are guidelines when the item has a stain: Never spend very much on a stained garment. If the shopowner insists that the stain will come out easily, you'll have to ask yourself why he didn't remove the stain himself. You might agree to buy the item or even pay an extra $5, if he removes the stain for you first.

If he won't do that, get the price down to a level where you can comfortably take a chance on the garment. Think twice about a stain on a colored item. Many treatments that will remove the stain will also fade the fabric around it. If that happens, is there some way you can cover the area? Is it small enough for a brooch, or in a location where a fabric flower (or other trim) would be appropriate?

If you know what the fabric content is and you know what the stain is, then follow the guidelines in books on fabric care and stain-removal (see References). If you don't know what the stain is, and if the fabric is a mystery, I'd advise that you check with a couple of collectors or shopowners. If they can't make recommendations, check with a local Home Ec teacher, your county extension agent, or a dry cleaner. And you can always write to customer service departments of cleaning product manufacturers.

What do I do? This is not to be interpreted as advice, because every stain and every fabric is different. I check to see if the fabric is washable, by moistening an inside seam allowance or another area that won't show. If it doesn't discolor with water, then I try water plus the soap I'm planning to use. This is usually diluted Basic H. Once I've determined that the fabric can be washed safely, I test the cleaning products. A very dilute solution of hydrogen peroxide can do wonders for stains on white fabrics. I buy the dilute solution at the pharmacy, and then add just a small amount to a bowl of water. Sometimes I have to leave the garment in the solution for awhile.

Friends of mine swear by presoak of an all-fabric bleach such as Clorox II. Others recommend a paste of an enzyme cleaner such as Axion, or an old-time enzyme treatment: buttermilk. I've also had success with cleaning products by Van Wyck. One of them, Perma Press, removed a blood stain from some Victorian drawers. The stain had been there for at least 50 years and could not be removed by any other product in my laundryroom.

Hairspray does seem to remove ballpoint pen ink when used as a laundry pretreatment. Select an inexpensive hairspray that contains no perfume. A pump-style bottle is better than an aerosol because you can open the bottle and apply the hairspray directly to the stain. A cotton swab is a good applicator for this.

Ordinary club soda removes certain stains and is less likely to mar fabric than some chemicals. Check stain-removal guides for its use.

An unusual treatment for white clothing was offered by a member of a New England audience during one of my lectures. The woman said that if a stain remained after washing a white garment, the item should be placed in the sun on top of a clean snowbank. I've heard about this sunbleaching method — and variations of it — from several people since then. The garment should be wet when it is placed in the sun, according to most reports.

Never try to remove a stain unless the garment is unwearable while the stain remains. No matter what the recommendations, a cleaner may discolor or damage the fabric. Never use a cleaner unless you are prepared for this to happen. Consult as many experts on stain removal as you can before using any chemical treatment.

If all else fails, you can always sell the garment to someone else. I know dealers who will buy anything I bring them, though they may pay me very little. I have friends who are fabric artists and desperately need unwearable garments. They cut them up for their own works of art. And there are always auction houses that will take stained or damaged clothes because a button-buyer will want them. Or some equally hopeful vintage clothing buyer will take a chance on the garments. And maybe she will know the secret of getting the stains out.

Buy clothing that you'll love. Shop and bid intelligently, so that you get the best deals. Don't buy anything that needs work, unless you're certain that you can handle it. If you take a chance on a stained or shredding garment, be prepared for a disappointment now and then. Treat auctions, and buying in general, as a game, and above all, have fun.

Diana Venegas, a professional designer, adds vintage elegance to her romantic contemporary clothing. Photo courtesy of Diana Venegas.

CHAPTER 8

Collecting Vintage
and Antique Clothing

After you've read the previous chapter on wearables, you're ready to start buying. However, the finer details of collecting are described in this chapter, and you should review these before spending large amounts. I will be talking about vintage and antique clothing, because many collectors use these terms to distinguish the age of the items. *Vintage* most often refers to old twentieth-century clothing. *Antique* means any clothing made before 1900. Some collectors prefer *vintage* to describe clothing that is less than 100 years old. When talking with others about old clothing, it is smart to define your terms so that you clearly understand each other.

First let me warn you: Collecting clothing can become a full-time addiction. You may find yourself budgeting for it from each paycheck. Evenings and weekends are planned around rummage sales, auctions, and yard sales. Your car's weekly mileage soars as you drive hundreds of miles for vintage-clothing shows and flea markets where you've heard rumors of a great dealer. On trash day, you'll find yourself driving very slowly past houses that seem to be throwing out old items. Even dumpsters become fair game. In the early stages of "picking" (that is, salvaging wonderful items

Authentic clothing is worn by Mrs. Whitaker, the storekeeper's wife, and Mrs. Curtis, the blacksmith's wife, at Prairietown, Conner Prairie's 1836 historic village. Photo courtesy of Conner Prairie.

from other people's trash and castaways), you'll visit neighbor-hoods where you won't be recognized. In later stages of picking, you won't hesitate to rummage through the trash of your next-door neighbor.

Soon, you're visiting museum curators to learn about cli-mate-control devices for your closet, to keep your textiles in near-perfect condition. Instead of investing in a new car, you're order-ing custom-made shelving for your storage area. Next, the spare bedroom becomes "the gallery." You may find yourself wanting a new house for enough space to store and display your acquisitions. You promise to quit as soon as you have completed your nine-teenth-century bonnet collection, but then find yourself lingering over parasols. First a few parasols are stored in the corner of your closet, then suddenly you're haunting auctions for an 1890s green-and-purple carved-handle parasol. You start counting the years until the baby will be in college so you can have his room. Collect-ing clothing has become an obsession.

You have been warned!

USING PRICE GUIDES

Before you set out to buy, perhaps at an auction, you should be prepared. Bring your price guides. These are books, usually in pa-perback, which describe items sold at auctions, and for how much. You can buy these in many regular bookstores. A few titles are list-ed in the References section, but any book from Kovels that lists textiles is a reliable choice. One of the best by-mail sources for textile price guides is Joslin Hall Books (see Resources). Major auction houses such as Sotheby's often sell their catalogues by mail, but be certain to order the list of successful bids as well. The catalogue will be sent before the auction, and you'll receive the prices after the auction. Auction houses usually charge around $5 to $10 for this service. There are also magazines, such as *Price Guide to Antiques*, which list the latest selling prices for certain categories of antiques. During some months, they will list clothing items. Prices vary widely from area to area, and also from one year to the next. When you are collecting actively, it is wise to keep up-to-date. If you're collecting as an investment, it is vital.

I always pack current price guides and recent auction catalogues with the selling prices noted in the trunk of my car. At yard sales where an item is overpriced, I take out my books to show the seller, and have successfully brought the price down. At an auction, I'm not so eager to take out my books. As I said earlier, part of the game involves looking bored with particularly exciting items. So I won't gleefully flip through my price guide to find the same item which sold for thousands of dollars in New York. After all, someone else at the auction might discover the item's true identity, under all that dust and dirt. Instead, I recommend that you examine each item closely, making detailed notes and sketches as casually as you can manage. Maybe people will think you're a college student, studying costume.

Once you have completed your notes on all interesting items, go out to your car and read through your books. Compare descriptions and note prices. This gives you an idea of what to expect at bidding.

ASSESSING VALUE

If you don't know the fine points of collectible clothing, if you have little experience in your region, or if you don't know the interests of the competing bidders, the price guides can be nearly worthless. New England has so many antique clothes coming out of attics and basements they have become pretty ho-hum for most general antique dealers. However, New England also has many collectors who will bid high when necessary. Prices will stay low when no other collectors are in the audience, or if the quality of the items doesn't meet their standards. In Florida I haven't seen many antique clothes, but I also haven't seen many people who care about them, so there is generally little competition, though the supply is low.

Quality can be a key. A shoe with its original box may sell for ten times what the shoe would, alone. A convincing copy in excellent condition can sell far higher or lower than the mediocre original, depending upon the buyers. Auctions will be an educational experience, as you learn to judge items and buyers.

How can you tell a copy? The easiest way is to know your materials. Homespun was more widely available than machine-made textiles until the early nineteenth century. Of course, plenty of people today weave their own fabrics, so you cannot immediately date a homespun garment as pre-Civil War. And high-quality homespun is difficult to recognize, since it can be as smooth as many of today's factory-made fabrics.

Sewing machines were patented in France in 1830, and in the U.S. in 1846. They were not in general use for about 20 years. Then, suddenly, sewing machines were extremely popular. So a machine-made garment was probably sewn after 1860. In some cases, the early sewing machines had rough, uneven stitches that look nearly the same as the perfect handsewing of that era. If you have some doubt, look closely. The telltale sign is often the knot where the thread was first inserted, in handsewing.

If you can find a loose end to a thread, you can sometimes guess the authenticity of a garment. In the eighteenth century, nearly all thread used for garments was homespun linen. This was followed by three-ply cotton thread in the nineteenth and early twentieth centuries. Six-ply cotton thread was available from about 1840 on. (The *ply* is the number of individual threads that are twisted together to make the bigger thread (Fig. 8–1).

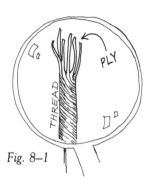

Fig. 8–1

For print dresses, I recommend consulting a book called *Quilts in America* by Patsy and Myron Orlofsky (see References). This book was published in 1974, and it is difficult to find today: Inter-library loan will be your best chance. It gives information on dating textiles, especially by fabric print and pattern. Of course, this book is about quilts and specifically those in America, so the scope is limited, but it is still one of the best references for dating textiles.

Obviously, synthetic fabrics are of recent vintage. If you cannot recognize synthetics and synthetic blends by touch, go to a large fabric store and compare the way that fabrics feel. You only need distinguish synthetics and blends as a category from fabrics with 100 percent natural fibers. You don't need to know 60/40 blends from 80/20, or Orlon from Dacron. Then "test" yourself by going to a clothing store: Can you tell synthetics and blends by touch and sight? There is often a difference in color quality and texture in fabrics containing synthetic fibers.

Zippers are another giveaway. First of all, you won't find them in Colonial and Civil War garments. Zippers were first patented for fastening shoes in 1893, and didn't appear in clothing until the twentieth century. Nylon zippers are from the last couple of decades, if you're looking for an authentic early twentieth-century garment. However, I have seen broken metal zippers replaced by recent nylon ones in repaired early twentieth-century garments. This is the sort of thing that makes dating difficult: A garment was not a collectible when it was simply out-of-fashion or wearing out. The owner might have refurbished older clothes to make the wearable; you'll find evidence of several eras in these garments.

A magnifying glass can be useful in determining thread ply and for closely studying fibers in a garment. Above all, wash your hands before handling textiles. If you have your eye on a particular item, you may want to guard it if food is being served at the auction. (It is common for a concession to be set up at auctions. This can be hazardous to your prospective purchases.) Of course, if you are too protective of an item, you're revealing your interest in it. You may want to point out the hazard to the staff at the auction, letting them know that you will bid on a particular item only if it is not stained during the preview. However, experienced auction-goers are pros at handling items carefully, and juggling food and beverages at the same time. I've watched a man with a cigarette in his mouth place a full coffee cup in the crook of his elbow, and pick up a magnificent beaded dress to examine. The ash didn't fall and the coffee stayed in the cup. You'll see this sort of thing, and you'll develop nerves of steel. You'll also learn to recognize the careless amateur who is a real threat to your planned purchases. Those are the people to point out to the auction staff. They jeopardize other items in the preview besides "your" treasured clothing. So, be careful when you're examining items. You may be asked to buy an item you damage for the highest price in the price guides. You may also be denied admission to future auctions.

If you are an amateur, watch to see which people at the preview seem to know what they're doing. A pro in textiles will give you many valuable pointers. When you see her looking at an item that you admire, saunter over and say, "What do you think of it?". A pro will often give you a rundown, such as, "Well, the lining is shot [this means the silk has been weighted with a treatment that is destroying the fibers; another term for the same damage is "shattered"] but the dress itself is still wearable. It has no moth damage, but repairs are needed along the shoulder seams and there is a small tear at the waist. The hooks are there but the eyes are missing. It needs some repair and you'd have to pull the lining [remove it], but it's good for a cheap wearable or costume. Maybe $20, tops." If the pro is seriously interested in buying the item, the description will be less flattering and the recommended bid price (if any is mentioned) will be lower, to keep you from recognizing the item's true value. Even with this misleading advice, you'll learn things that you'd have missed otherwise. A less helpful pro, or someone who sees you as a competitor, will mutter something like, "It's okay," and that's all. However, enough friendly auction-goers will help you learn. Many remember when they were beginners, too.

LOCATING COLLECTIBLES

Chapter 7 covered the purchase of wearables, but as a *collector*, you'll be in a slightly different setting. At elite auctions, you'll be competing with a far more cutthroat crowd than at the auctions where costumes and wearables are usually purchased. Of course, it is possible to buy collectibles at a yard sale or a small auction; however, if you become a serious collector, you'll also shop at the major auction houses, such as Sotheby's. And that crowd is playing with far more money, on far less friendly terms, than the casual auction-goers I discussed earlier.

Some auction houses classify clothing as *collectibles*, while others feature them in their auctions as *antiques*. They also vary the categories where clothing is listed. Check these headings for mention of clothing: Accessories, Attire, Clothing, Costumes, Fashions, Fabric pieces, Garments, Household goods, Textiles, Wearables, and the all-purpose Miscellaneous.

On my first visit to a "real" auction, I was glad that I assumed my usual place in the back of the hall. That way, I could sneak out when it became apparent that I was over my head. At this particular auction, the crowd was practically in black tie, while I was in my usual faded blue jeans. (But I could justify my old-fashioned,

Price guides and catalogs →

Dressy jacket →

← clean hands

← Magnifying glass

←"Vintage" blue jeans

Fig. 8-2

button-front Levis. After all, they are reproductions of historical clothing, too.)

If I don't know what to expect at an auction, I may throw a change of clothing into the trunk of my car. Or wear "good" blue jeans with a nice blouse, and carry a stylish blazer to dress it up if necessary. While I won't blend in with the little-black-dress-and-pearls set, my dignity isn't quite so bruised as when I'm clearly underdressed. You'll be comfortable in blue jeans at about 90 percent of the auctions you'll attend. Auction merchandise is often as dusty as it emerged from the barn, attic, or basement where it was stored. As soon as you've rummaged through one box lot, you're ready for a good bath.

Sometimes, if you dress as if you don't have much money, you can bluff your way through the preview, since you'll be discounted as someone who can't afford to bid high anyway. This is one reason why many dealers dress in workclothes, too. At the "elegant" auctions, the situation can be quite different. Dress to the teeth. Look as though you can afford to bid *forever* to claim the item that you want. And if the concession offers complimentary vintage champagne, brace yourself for high selling prices.

I have been over my head at country auctions under a tent. And I've picked up wonderful pieces for under $25 at more formal auctions. However, if the auction house is fancy, and the catalogues are on nice paper with plenty of illustrations, then the auction house expects to make a good profit. That's how they stay in business, and afford such nice "extras." And they won't make big profits on box lots that sell for $20 or less.

If you're a serious collector, you'll find many of the best-documented items at elite auctions. A smart seller with a valuable item wants the best price she can get. If you're zealously collecting, the mint-condition 1814 bonnet may be exactly what you need, and you'll be willing to pay dearly just to complete your collection. (If this concept eludes you, think about completing a jigsaw puzzle or the crosswords. The collector who needs only two more bonnets to have one for every fashion trend of the nineteenth century will bid until he claims those two bonnets.)

By contrast, if a garment turns out to be insignificant to the collectors at one of these elite auctions, the item may go for less than it would have at a small, country auction. The serious collector will save every cent until his item comes up for bid. Serious

Collecting Vintage and Antique Clothing

collectors will also purchase advertisements in publications that sellers might read. And they'll keep those ads running for years. When I lived in New England, I had an ad in many bargain-shopper publications, offering to buy certain items at certain prices. Yes, I was offering a price that would have insulted many people, but I also received plenty of calls from eager sellers. Many though that I was absolutely crazy to pay so much for something that they "knew" to be trash. Many times, I told them exactly how to sell the item elsewhere, for several times my offer. Not one seller was interested in going elsewhere for more money. If my ad offered $20 for nineteenth-century parasols in any condition, they wanted the $20.

When you're in an antique shop, be certain to ask about the items that most interest you. They may be in the "junk box" under the counter, or in the back room.

Collectors also find the best selection at vintage clothing shows. These shows are similar to any antique show, with row after row of tables set up, selling vintage and antique clothing and accessories. Some are run for one day, others last two or three days. Some dealers will haggle over prices, especially on the last day. Others are convinced that they will get full price back at their shop, or at the next vintage clothing show. Many dealers travel across the country to have a table at a good vintage clothing show. One of the best shows in the country is produced by Molly's/Grandmother's Vintage Clothing Promotions (see Resources). This show is usually held twice a year, near Auburn, Massachusetts, and dealers from all over the country have magnificent displays of vintage and antique clothes. To learn about major shows throughout the U.S. and Canada, read the quarterly newsletter, "Molly's/Grandmother's Vintage Gazette." Some antiques magazines, such as *Hobbies* will list shows including textiles and clothing, too.

When friends and acquaintances know that you are a collector, they will often offer you items from a relative's estate. It makes Esmeralda feel good to know that Aunt Mabel's white lace petticoat is being cherished as part of your collection. However, Esmeralda may be horrified if she sees you wearing Aunt Mabel's white lace petticoat as a skirt, in a casual setting.

If you receive a gift from someone, be certain that you understand how they expect you to use it. If they expect you to wear it,

Fig. 8–3

be certain they'll see you in it at some time in the near future. If you are supposed to place the item in acid-free tissue paper, in a cedar-lined closet (assuming that you have all these at hand), do not horrify them by pointing out the pieces of the garment in your new patchwork vest, á la Ralph Lauren. And if you need acid-free paper, cedar for your closet, or other special items for storage, check with your nearest art museum for local sources.

CARING FOR COLLECTIBLES

Cleaning

Cleaning and laundering has been discussed in the section on wearables. However, for valuable collectibles that cannot risk damage, I recommend that you contact antique dealers in your area. Ask several for their suggestions about trustworthy dry cleaners. Most antique dealers do not recommend any cleaning beyond brushing off dust and dirt, and for that chore they often suggest a soft-bristled paintbrush. However, let's assume that you have an item that is not a museum-quality piece, and it is safe to dry clean.

Another way to locate a good dry cleaner is to ask at the most expensive men's shop in town. From time to time, a customer may stain a garment while trying it on, and then refuse to buy it. The store must depend on a reliable dry cleaner to carefully restore the garment to "like new" condition, so that it can be sold to someone else.

When you take a garment to a dry cleaner, make certain that the piece has been appraised and is covered by your household insurance policy. Your insurance agent can help you with this. Then be certain that your dry cleaner knows how to handle antique textiles. Ask precisely what precautions he will take. Be sure that his insurance covers damage he may do, in *full replacement value*. Find out what documentation would be necessary, and be certain that you have it. Once you find a good dry cleaner, work with him closely when soiled items can be safely dry cleaned. Don't risk your treasured items when you have any question about their safety.

In many cases, antique clothing cannot be safely dry cleaned. I know of no remedy for this problem. Accept the dirt and stains as part of the item's history.

CROCHET TULIP-BAG.

BY MRS. JANE WEAVER.

THIS small bag need not be made of any expensive material, and therefore Alpine pink and a middle shade of green single Berlin wool can be used, with the edges worked in gold twine. If, however, it is made for a purse, then middle size netting silk and fine gold twist should be substituted.

A small steel tassel, Penelope needle No. 3, and 2 yards of fine wire, will be required.

THE TULIP, FIRST PETAL.—Commence with the pink wool, *, make 31 chain; and for the

1st or center round—Turn, miss 3, 23 treble, 3 plain, turn, 1 chain to cross, and up the other side; and for the

2nd round—6 plain, 17 treble, 2 treble in 1 stitch, 1 treble (2 treble in one, 5 times), turn, and down the other side, 1 treble, 2 treble in one, 12 treble, 6 plain, 1 single on the 1 chain that crosses; and for the

3rd round—1 single, 8 plain, 15 treble, 2 treble in one, 2 treble, 2 treble in one, 1 treble (2 treble in one, 4 times), 1 treble, 2 treble in one, 2 treble, 2 treble in one, 15 treble, 8 plain, 1 single. Repeat from * 5 times more, join on the gold twist or silk, and work 1 single on the 1st plain stitch of the 1st petal; then round the six petals thus—

THE EDGE ROUND.—Take the wire and work it under the stitches, 25 plain (2 plain in one, and 1 plain, 8 times), 2 plain in one, ** 25 plain, 1 single, then up the next petal, 1 single on the 1st stitch, 5 plain, join to the 6th stitch of the 1st petal, counting from the last stitch, 6 plain, join to the 6th stitch of the 1st petal, always counting from the last joining, 7 plain, join to the 7th stitch of the 1st petal, 6 plain (2 plain in one, and 1 plain, 8 times), 2 plain in one. Repeat from ** 4 times more; then to make it round, 6 plain, join to the 19th stitch of the 1st petal, 7 plain, join to the 12th stitch of the 1st petal, 6 plain, join to the 6th stitch of the 1st petal, 5 plain, 1 single; cut off the wire, twisting the ends together to secure it, work along the ends of the petals (3 chain and 1 plain in the 1 chain between the petals, 6 times), (1 chain, and 1 plain in the 3 chain, 6 times). Fasten off.

FOR THE LINING.—Commence with the green wool or silk, work 114 chain, make it round by working a treble stitch in the 1st chain stitch.

1st round—2 chain, miss 2, 1 treble. Repeat all round, and work 19 rounds more the same, join on the gold.

Storage

Never store your textiles in plastic bags. Fabric needs to breathe. It will rot more quickly in an air-tight environment. If you must store your clothing in some sort of bag, use a clean, washed, white pillowcase or sheet of 100 percent cotton.

Do not hang up antique clothing. Those old fashions were heavy, and they will be stressed when their full weight is suspended on a coat hanger. Drawers are ideal, if they are designed to hold garments with few folds. Drawers such as these are described in *Collecting Costume* by Naomi Tarrant (see References).

If you must hang your clothing, I recommend that you purchase several sizes of plastic hangers. Victorian dresses often had very narrow shoulders, which would be stretched on today's hangers. Locate tubular plastic hangers intended for children's clothes. Some collectors object to plastic hangers, fearing that they give off a gas that is harmful to fabric. I've heard the same concerns about the chemicals used to treat wood hangers. Wire hangers need careful padding, and you should use cotton for this because plain cotton batting does not give off any risky gasses. In my own closet, I use tubular plastic hangers.

Over the plastic hangers, you place a padding and a cover. Cotton batting is available at quilting supply stores, and is the best padding for coat hangers. The cover for the coat hanger and padding should also be of 100 percent cotton. Wash it thoroughly, particularly if you are using a colored or printed fabric.

Beaded gowns and other extremely heavy garments should not be hung under any circumstances.

Pants and slacks should be folded over a well-padded hanger. A clip-style hanger will leave indentations in the cuffs or waistband.

When hanging clothes, pay special attention to any surface treatment of the garments. Decorative buttons, hooks, and beading can catch on surfaces next to them. Be certain that they will not snag a nearby garment. If you cover each garment with a sheet or pillowcase, be careful when removing it, so that the hooks and such aren't caught in the cover.

Your clothing should never come in contact with wood surfaces. Use acid-free tissue paper, which is often available at artists' supply shops (see Resources for mail-order sources).

Our full-sized pattern, this month, is that of the *Pardessus Danois*. The pattern consists of three pieces, namely, the top part of back and front, our paper not allowing us to give the full length, and the sleeve. In giving the full length to the pattern, the *middle* of back must be 37¼ inches from the top to the bottom; the edge of front must be 30½ inches, and the length of side seam 23 inches. In the sleeve, the seam at the back of the arm is left open at the bottom as far as the notch: this style of sleeve is in great favor, as is also the wide pagoda. This *Pardessus* is generally made in the same material as the dress, the trimming to correspond. The lengths we have given are for a lady of medium height, and they may have to be slightly increased or reduced as required by the height of the wearer.

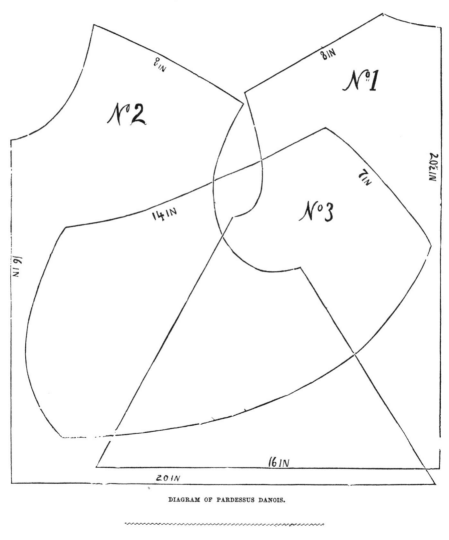

DIAGRAM OF PARDESSUS DANOIS.

Herbal insect repellents are safer than mothballs. The loose sachet is available at Crabtree & Evelyn, and small ready-to-store bags of herbal repellent are sold by several sources, including The Vermont Country Store mail-order catalogue (see Resources). The authors of *Quilts in America* recommend the herb southernwood (*Artemisia arbotanum*).

Whenever your garments are folded, pad the inside of the fold with tissue paper, so that the crease is softened. In addition, you should refold the garment every couple of months, or you may find it permanently creased. The crease will become dry and brittle in time, and that is where the fabric will first deteriorate.

If the garment has padding and is stored flat, you should use acid-free tissue paper to fill the area around the padding. Victorian garments often had shoulder and/or chest padding. This padding will stick out, creating a crease, if the surrounding garment is left flat without support.

A perfectly flat garment may be rolled on a large tube. Small garments may fit on a regular mailing tube. You'll find much longer cardboard tubes at upholstery and fabric shops. Some will give or sell you these empty tubes. Some carpeting also comes on these large cardboard tubes.

The garment must be protected from the surface of the tube with an acid-free paper. Some books recommend covering the tube with aluminum foil first, and then covering the foil with acid-free paper. Tissue paper or pure white cotton should be rolled with the garment, so that the layers are separated. Also, if the garment has any pleats or gathers in it, you will be pressing the creases into the garment by rolling it. Rolling is recommended only for flat items such as shawls, veils, and some kimono-like garments. You would never roll a padded garment, such as one with shoulder pads, or one with surface treatment, such as beading. It is better to store all items as flat as possible; rolling is only suggested where space is a consideration, or when it is a safer way to transport garments.

Some small items, such as lace and trim, can be wrapped around a small tubular core of cardboard. Several of these can be stored in a paper-lined drawer or box. Clothing should never be stored in direct sunlight. It will fade.

Wherever you store your clothing, be certain to keep the area as clean and dust-free as possible. It is also wise to check for insects regularly.

Repairs

With any textile, you must make a choice: You can do your best to conceal a repair, just as if you had been its original owner; or you can repair it in such a way as to make the repair obvious, so that no one is misled about the condition of the costume or the era of its repairs.

If you're going to conceal the repair, you can use contemporary materials or seek out antiques. I prefer to use antiques as much as possible, but I haven't had consistent success with antique thread. Too often, it is weak or brittle. Instead, I use new 100 percent cotton thread in a matching color, or a cotton blend thread if I cannot match the color with a pure cotton. My sewing needles are tiny Clovers, intended for quilting. They leave a tiny hole in the fabric, no larger than the thread. See the Resources section for mail-order sources of Clover needles and cotton thread.

Buttons, hooks and eyes, and even fabric can be purchased in many general antique shops. I stock up on these items at auctions, for future needs. Some fabric shops carry antique buttons, too.

If you prefer to make the repair obvious, you should use a good grade of pure cotton for the replacement fabric. Other materials should be clearly new, but complementary to the garment. Gentle basting stitches are fine if the area will not be under stress.

To conceal a hole in fabric, you may need to visit a tailor for reweaving. Some firms can effectively repair holes in sweaters. If you can knit or crochet, you can often find old yarn or crochet thread at yard sales and rummage sales, to repair garments authentically. It is rare to match a knit garment exactly.

No matter what repairs you make when you purchase an item, time takes its toll on textiles. Continue to make repairs as long as the garment serves your needs. However, at some point, the clothing may deteriorate beyond value as a collectible. Never discard antique clothing. First, check local museums and collections, in case they would like the garment, even in a state of decay. If they do, your donation may be tax-deductible.

If you don't find a new owner for the garment, see how much of it can be salvaged. The buttons, hooks and eyes, and any other trim should be placed in your collection for future use. Pieces of the fabric may be used later, to repair other garments. If you don't use antique fabric for your repairs, check with local quilting groups. Many quilters would be thrilled to use antique fabrics in their quilts and fabric art.

No matter what its condition, every antique garment has something of value. Old-fashioned clothes are an endangered species. Treat them well.

LADIES' ANKLET.

BY EMILY H. MAY.

 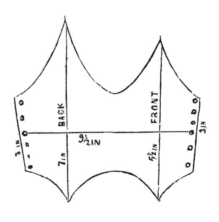

WE vary our department, this month, by giving a pattern and diagram for a lady's anklet, a useful article just coming into fashion. The anklet is to be worn just above the boot, and is made of kid, lined with flannel, the whole bound with galloon. Where it fastens on the outside of the ankle, it may either have eyelets put in, and laced on buttons and loops of gum elastic.

We give a diagram of the anklet with the dimensions to fit a lady of medium size.

THE NAIM CLOAK.

BY EMILY H. MAY.

Our diagram, this month, is of a fashionable cloak, called The Naim Cloak in Paris. An engraving of the cloak is given above. It is a paletot pattern and is made short. The material may be either cloth, velvet, or thick silk. The ornaments consist of binding arranged in arabesques.

No. 1. FRONT OF CLOAK.
No. 2. SIDE.

No. 3. ONE HALF OF BACK.
No. 4. SLEEVE.

Those who copy this pattern must be careful to lengthen the side 30 C, (12 inches) from the places marked with crosses, following the bias, in order to have sufficient length and fulness. The same must be done with No. 3 back, except that it must be lengthened 45 C (18 inches), from the crosses.

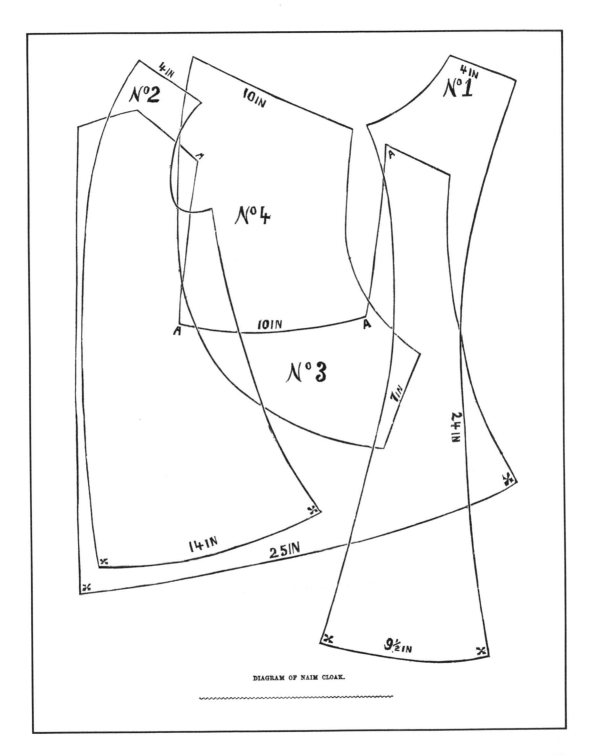

DIAGRAM OF NAIM CLOAK.

CHAPTER 9

Something Old, Something New

I f you are a purist, this is another chapter to skip. If you believe that antiques belong in museums and private collections, this chapter will infuriate you. If you think that fashion eras should never be mixed, it will turn you pale. This chapter is for (irreverent?) women who want to add historical touches to their present-day wardrobes.

In your mind, you see yourself in elegant fashions of the past. Your company expects you in smart office attire. How can you compromise? There are gradients to wearing old-fashioned clothes. You might start with a touch of nostalgic costume and work your way up. At some point, you'll reach a level which is as daring as you can be without losing your job. This will vary with the situation, your courage, and your personal creativity.

The princess-style gowns and veiled hats of the Medieval era are a bit difficult to modify for office wear. In fact, they're usually limited to organizations such as Society for Creative Anachronism (see Clubs, Organizations, Periodicals section), and for costume wear. However, several companies produce wonderful jewelry from the Middle Ages. Raymond's Quiet Press has accent pieces that will hold a cape in place nicely. (All companies mentioned here are listed in Resources.) In fact, any of their jewelry can be

Armistice blouse, Folkwear pattern from Times Past. Photo by Jerry Wainwright, courtesy of Folkwear.

Fig. 9–1

Fig. 9–2

Fig. 9–3

dazzling when combined with simple contemporary fashions. The idea is to draw attention to the jewelry.

If your taste is Colonial, you could accent your usual office wear with a scoop-necked blouse and tuck in a solid-colored kerchief. A fitted vest over a chemise-style blouse can look stylish but conservative when worn with a basic, gathered skirt. You might even baste and embroidered pocket to your waistband.

If Regency is your era, you can create wonderful outfits that reflect the romance of Jane Austen. The Regency pattern from the Wisconsin State Historical Society can be made into a great blouse; I made mine with heavy, paisley cotton intended for upholstery, and added a delicate silk collar. A simple, gathered skirt in a matching solid color turns it into an elegant ensemble. Bonnets from that era are also very practical for cold winter days. You can buy patterns for bonnets, or you an get a head start with a basic bonnet form from Amazon or Dazian. If you want to make truly spectacular bonnets, write to the Wonderful World of Hats for their information.

Women with a taste for Civil War era clothing can use the bodices of patterns from Heidi Marsh and others, to create delightful blouses (Fig. 9–2). The embroidered, suspender-like straps might be a bit much for the office, and hoop skirts generally do not fit in the openings under desks.

Maybe you prefer late Victorian and early Edwardian fashions (Figs. 9–3 and 9–4). Your first step is to wear a few accent pieces influenced by the past. Some jewelry companies specialize in old-fashioned items, such as cameos. You might tie your hair back with a strip of elegant lace. (Of course, you don't want to ruin gorgeous antique lace with oil from your hair. Keep in mind how fragile actual antique pieces are when you plan to wear them.)

Next, shop for some separates that have old-fashioned styling. A first choice might be a back-buttoned blouse with a high, lacy, Victorian collar. You can go a step further, and browse through unusual pattern catalogues, such as those from Folkwear. They often illustrate ethnic and old-fashioned separates, combined for a very contemporary look. Your look will be unique, but few will guess the origin of the clothing.

Sew old-fashioned buttons and trim on your contemporary clothing. If you make your own clothing, you can take the yoke from an actual high-collared Victorian garment, and sew it into a

Fig. 9–4

Edwardian dinner gown

contemporary dress. Of course, you'd only do this if the rest of the antique garment were unwearable.

You can be bolder, and wear an outfit that is a modified version of fashions from the past. For example, Folkwear's easy Victo-

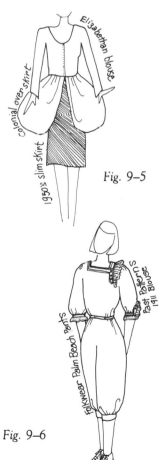

Elizabethan blouse

Colonial over skirt

1950's slim skirt

Fig. 9–5

Fig. 9–6

Past Patterns 1911 Blouse

Folkwear Palm Beach pants

Diana Venegas, a professional designer, adds vintage elegance to her romantic contemporary clothing. Photo courtesy of Diana Venegas.

127

Something Old, Something New

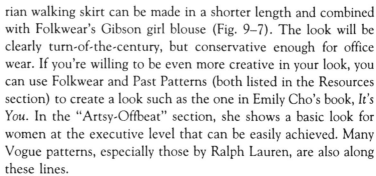

Fig. 9–7

Fig. 9–8

rian walking skirt can be made in a shorter length and combined with Folkwear's Gibson girl blouse (Fig. 9–7). The look will be clearly turn-of-the-century, but conservative enough for office wear. If you're willing to be even more creative in your look, you can use Folkwear and Past Patterns (both listed in the Resources section) to create a look such as the one in Emily Cho's book, *It's You*. In the "Artsy-Offbeat" section, she shows a basic look for women at the executive level that can be easily achieved. Many Vogue patterns, especially those by Ralph Lauren, are also along these lines.

As your courage builds, combine sleeves from the more elegant and dramatic Past Patterns, with simple blouse patterns. Some of their Edwardian patterns have detailing that would look spectacular on a simple dress or blouse.

Your taste in clothing, the occasion, and the impression you must make will all dictate how much historical and antique clothing you want to mix with contemporary apparel. But even if you wear a uniform to work, you'll find little ways to include touches from your favorite era. It just takes a little ingenuity, and careful study of the details in past fashions.

Fig. 9–9

Early American shirt

Regency blouse

Edwardian blouse

Colonial pocket

Beaded bag

Victorian walking skirt

1930's slim skirt

1950's bias-cut skirt

A few mix 'n' match possibilities

Fig. 9–10

129
Something Old, Something New

CHAPTER 10
Ideas for Writers

Even though you may never sew the clothing you mentally "construct," you'll still follow the same basic research steps as a costume designer. Look through the books I've recommended in References. Some modern books give insight into the clothing, while others are merely colorful, slightly inaccurate, whisks through history. My recommendations include the books that I have on my reference shelf, but hundreds of books have been published in the last couple of centuries which give excellent information about historical fashions. The best resources are those published *during* the era. The Victorian book, *What Every Young Woman Should Know*, is likely to be a better source than a modern interpretation. Books on manners can be invaluable resources. For example, they may tell you how the gown was carried when climbing stairs, when to speak to a single man, or the correct way to use a fan.

Diaries are also gems for writers. They give insight into the daily lives of your characters. You'll discover what people did with their clothing when they went to bed, how garments were cleaned, how often a gown was worn or restyled, and how long it took to make a garment. These old books are often available through the

Romance writers Janet Dailey, left, and Barbara Cartland, right, with Kathryn Falk, owner of Romantic Times Publishing Group.

Fig. 10–1

booksellers listed in the Resources section. Some companies, such as R. L. Shep, are reprinting the best of the old fashion books.

By contrast, if you're writing about ancient history, read the most recent books. New discoveries are constantly being made, so don't trust some early-twentieth-century book on the subject. The earlier books may have more details, but they'll also include more speculation. Above all, study illustrated histories that show the art of the time. Look closely at the styles in paintings of your era, then read notes about those particular paintings for current interpretations.

However, reading alone isn't enough. You may have accurate information about the time, but your writing isn't likely to have the full, rich color of the period. And in fiction, your readers usually want plenty of color and detailing.

Make or buy a few reproductions of the garments of your characters. They say that a picture is worth a thousand words; let's revise that to say that a real, physical example can *lend* a thousand words to your writing—in lush and accurate descriptions! Dressing a doll in the clothing can be sufficient. However, I've learned a tremendous amount about historical clothes by wearing them.

For example, the wooden-stayed corset of the mid to late eighteenth century made it nearly impossible to sit down comfortably. After wearing one, I suddenly understood why portraits often show a woman perched on the edge of her sofa. The stays stuck out over the shoulder blades, making the Polonaisse gown a necessity for a natural-looking back.

When I wore my heavy Victorian gowns with appropriate, multiple undergarments, I saw why high-top boots were a good idea. With the weight of the clothing, it was easy to turn an ankle when descending steep stairs that I couldn't see beneath my wide skirts.

Most writers want to fill their books with rich, accurate descriptions. You'll create these descriptions from firsthand study, if you actually wear the clothing of the time. Instead of copying the same old phrases about the sound of a gown, you'll find new words to describe the rustles and whispers you've heard personally. When your heroine climbs into her carriage, you'll know exactly how much work it was to lift her skirts gracefully to step up into the carriage.

It will also lend humor to your book if you wear the clothing in a variety of situations. I learned firsthand the hazards of a bodice that was fastened at the front with the large hooks of the Colonial period. To put it discreetly, they come unhooked when using both arms to carry things. A strategically placed pin is a good idea. This may be the reason for the pinned-on bib aprons of that era.

Victorian clothing can be equally ridiculous. Imagine being unable to fit through a doorway with a hoop skirt. Study your doorways well, before attempting to pass through them. (My personal downfall was a Victorian party in a reconstructed Medieval castle, with narrow little doorways.) It can be equally embarrassing to try to sit gracefully when the hoops just won't stay down. It is not an exaggeration to say that you can be hit in the teeth with a flying hoop. And it is often impossible to wedge into an armchair in Victorian clothing.

If you're writing a "bodice ripper" and it actually includes ripping the bodice, think the actions through. In eras of heavy thread, coarsely woven fabrics, and sewing techniques intended to last through years of daily wear, he would have been a very strong and determined man! Even those ethereal tea gowns of the Edwardian years were often made of silk. Silk wears like steel, and is about as easy to tear. A poorly made gown might rip accidentally, but that was the mark of a careless dressmaker.

Another detail I've clarified through personal experience is how long it takes to get dressed and undressed in historical clothing. It takes me ten minutes to unlace my high-top boots — and that's when I'm in a hurry. Corsets can be equally time-consuming, and your heroine would have to take it off, or at least unlace it, even for a brief nap. Corsets not only limit how deeply you can breathe, but they also jab uncomfortably without warning.

Of course, you can exaggerate all of this to create a ridiculous scene, as well. If your heroine is housecleaning, she'll have to change her entire outfit to go out for a carriage ride with your hero. If he calls on her unexpectedly and she has to change her clothing hastily to receive him, she may have to leave her workshoes on. I can imagine her walking with her knees slightly bent, to ensure that her skirt brushed the floor and concealed the embarrassing shoes. If she was a practical miss, she might not have worn a corset when housecleaning, and not have time to get laced in when hastily dressing for the hero. If the hero puts his arm around her in an unexpected moment of passion, he might have quite a surprise when he discovers that she is not confined in a corset.

You'll deliberately overlook the facts at times, for that perfect, romantic moment. In fiction, he really can rip her gown with ease. Hightop shoes and corsets fairly fly off when necessary. Fiction is fun. If a reader wanted the unadorned truth, she'd be reading the newspaper.

If you don't have the time, resources, or inclination to wear the clothing yourself, talk with those who do. Nearly every era has a club or organization, or a living history site where the correct fashions are being worn. Many of these modern-day firsthand sources are listed in *The Living History Sourcebook*. Museum staffers often know practical details, too. You'll find several excellent museums listed by state in *Textile, Costume, and Doll Collections*.

If you're going to write an historical novel, do your research well. Your audience craves the colorful details that make history, and your story, come alive. Read as much firsthand material as you can find, wear the clothing if you can, and create fresh descriptions for your eager readers.

Fig. 10–2

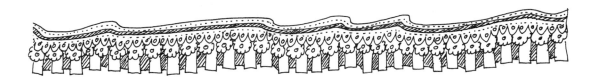

Afterword

Wearing historical clothing can be hilarious. I want to close with my favorite experience: It had been a long, full day of picture-taking. My children and I had our photos taken in Colonial clothing, for a Boston Tea Party ship exhibit. After several costume changes, and hours under hot studio lights, we didn't bother to change out of our Colonial garb to drive home.

We were on a busy Beacon Hill street when a traffic light in mid-block turned red. The car in front of me stopped at the crosswalk. I stopped smoothly behind him. The driver in back of me wasn't paying attention, and ran into the back of my car. The car rocked a bit, but the children didn't even know we'd been hit.

I swung open my door and stepped out to check for damage. The driver behind me was already out of his car, storming toward me angrily. In his fury, he'd forgotten to put down his opened beer can. He started to shout, "What do you think. . . ," but stopped mid-sentence. The color drained from his face.

In the excitement, I forgot that I was still in full Colonial garb. He looked as though he'd seen a ghost, and perhaps he thought that he had!

Then there were the cars. Mine is a model with those huge rubber bumper guards. His was a brand new car with a tiny bumper and fragile front grill. My car didn't have a scratch on it, while his entire grillwork had collapsed against the radiator.

Frankly, we were fine and my car had no damage, so the other driver had my sympathy. Apparently, my cheerful attitude was the last straw. I guess he couldn't believe he had done major damage to his own vehicle, yet the other car hadn't a scratch, and the driver seemed to be a cheerful ghost from the Revolution.

He apologized hastily, hopped into his car, and drove away quickly with his grillwork clanking. It was clear that the fright had sobered him, and I doubt that he'll ever drink and drive again!

Clothing from the past is fascinating. You'll learn so much that makes history come alive. It's even more fun to actually wear the fashions you've studied. You'll enjoy clothing more, whether you recreate the complete "look" of an era, or simply modify the fashions to add personal style to your daily wardrobe.

There is never a point when you know absolutely everything about clothing of an era. And many resources will contradict each other, making the mystery of fashion even more interesting than your favorite Sherlock Holmes stories.

Likewise, there is never a point where you will know all about every source for historical clothing. New sources appear and old ones go out of business. Since I'm as much a writer as I am a vintage-clothing buff, I hope you'll keep me up-to-date on new and favorite sources for vintage fashions.

If you have questions to ask or ideas to share, I hope that you'll write to me; include a self-addressed stamped envelope, so that I can answer you. Every aspect of historical fashions is fascinating to me, and I look forward to hearing from you.

My personal wish is that you find as much fun and excitement in historical fashions as I have.

Eileen MacIntosh
P.O. Box 688
Dunedin, FL 34697-0688

Resources

This listing includes the best sources of clothing, books, and related supplies for vintage and antique fashions. Companies and individuals are in alphabetical order, and the following code is used to designate eras of available merchandise:

G	=	General items, useful for several eras
M/R	=	Medieval and/or Renaissance
C	=	Colonial
Re	=	Regency
Ft	=	Fur Trade
V	=	Victorian
CW	=	Civil War
Ed	=	Edwardian

Centuries are noted in numerical form, 19th, 20th, etc.

If a letter is followed by parentheses, it means that the company specializes in the era/s in parentheses. Thus, G (V, CW) means general merchandise, specializing in Victorian and Civil War eras. The next series of letters, following a semicolon, indicate the particular types of merchandise:

V	=	Vintage and antique
P	=	Patterns
S	=	Sewing supplies
R	=	Readymade clothes
C	=	Custom-made clothes
A	=	Accessories
M/W/C	=	Clothing for men, women, and children
B	=	Books and publications
F	=	Footwear
O	=	Other special items
G	=	Guns or weapons
J	=	Jewelry
E	=	Just about everything you'll need for an era

Sample entry:

Amazon Dry Goods
2218 East 11th Street, Dept. VF
Davenport, IA 52803
G (19th); P, S, R, A, M/W/C, B, F, O, E
Catalogue: $2 for 19th-century items; $4 for hughe pattern list
    Amazon Dry Goods carries merchandise that can be used for several eras, but specializes in the nineteenth century. It carries patterns, sewing supplies, readymade clothing and accessories for men, women, and children. They sell books, footwear, and many other items of interest for the nineteenth century. In other words, they have nearly everything you'll need if you're portraying the Victorian or Civil War years.

1817 Shoppe
5606 State Rt. 37
Delaware, OH 43015
G; S
Catalogue: $3
    Natural fiber textiles, accurately reproduced from fabrics of the past. Homespun, ticking, blanket wool by the yard, and more.

Aardvark Territorial Enterprises
P.O. Box 2449
Livermore, CA 94550
G; S
Catalogue: $1 for mammoth issue
    The newspaper-style catalogue is more than a sales tool, it is one of the most inspiring networking vehicles in fabric art. Sewing supplies, books, and creative ideas fill their pages. Hard-to-find items, too.

Amazon Dry Goods
2218 East 11th Street, Dept. VF
Davenport, IA 52803
G (19th); P, S, R, A, M/W/C, B, F, O, E
Catalogue: $2 for 19th-century items; $4 for huge pattern list
    The $2 catalogue includes wonderful domestic items, books, sewing materials, and more. If you order only one Victorian catalogue, get this one. The pattern catalogue ($4) includes over 511 patterns from many different companies.

American Association for State and Local History (AASLH)
172 Second Avenue, North, Suite 102
Nashville, TN 37201
G
Catalogue: Send long SASE for information
   Books and other services for individuals, groups, and museums.

Aurora Silks
5806 N. Vancouver
Portland, OR 97217
G (20th); S, B
   Fabrics, yarns, and dyestuffs for accurate period clothing.

Barbara's
690 Island Way, #308
Clearwater, FL 34630
   Wearable period clothing and accessories of the romantic eras, up to the 1920s. Call for more information (813) 447-5679.

Barbara H. Clower, Books
2671 Cardinal Ridge Road
Charlottesville, VA 22901
B
Catalogue: $1
   Used and out-of-print books related to traditional arts and crafts of the home. Separate catalogue related to automobiles.

BeautiControl Cosmetics
P.O. Box 815189
Dallas, TX 75381-5189
G (contemporary); O
Catalogue: write for name of nearest consultant
   Free color consultation on best clothing and makeup colors.

Bette Feinstein
96 Roundwood Road
Newton, MA 02164
B
Catalogue: $1
   Old and antique books related to fabric arts, clothing, etiquette, and other delightful subjects. Out-of-print books, too.

Bjo Trimble
P.O. Box 36851
Los Angeles, CA 90036-0851
G; S
Catalogue: Send long SASE for information
     Bjo carries fine lace (up to ¾" wide) for trimming clothing, especially Victorian and Edwardian clothing. She will also search for any special items you need for your historical clothing and costumes.

Bonnet Brigade, The
38395 Alta Drive
Fremont, CA 94536
V, CW; R, A, M/W, B, O, G, F, E
Catalogue: $2
     Extensive supply of readymade items and patterns for the Civil War. Excellent prices.

Buffalo Enterprises of Pennsylvania
308 W. King St., P.O. Box 183
East Berlin, PA 17316
G
     Accessories and clothing.

Cabin Fever Calicoes
P.O. Box 54
Center Sandwich, NH 03227
G (contemporary); S
Catalogue: $2.75
     Remarkable catalogue of sewing supplies, mostly for quilters. High-quality notions to make sewing easier, including Clover needles. Enormous variety of solid color 100% cottons; swatches, $2.

Calico Corner, The
513 East Bowman Street
South Bend, IN 46613
V, CW; P, S, R, A, M/W, B, F
Catalogue: $2, refundable with purchase
     Cotton hoopskirts, crocheted gloves, mitts, snoods, purses, lace-up shoes, bonnets, parasols, patterns, mirrors, and other items for period living. Discounts to museums, park services, reenactors, for items purchased in quantity. Costuming workshops available, too.

Caroline Stitches in Time
21 Baron's Road, Rt. 2
Clemmons, NC 27012
G (18th–19th); P
Meticulously researched patterns including 18th and early-19th century everyday clothes.

Cerulean Blue, Ltd.
P.O. Box 21168
Seattle, WA 98111-3168
G (contemporary); S
Textile art supplies, including fabric dyes and books. The 1987 catalogue was $3.50.

Claire Molloy
23 Bow Road
Belmont, MA 02178
G (contemporary); O
Catalogue: write or call for information
Free color analysis to determine best colors for your historical clothing, and makeup that looks natural enough to wear in historical settings. The only makeup foundation that meets my standards for accuracy in appearance. (Common sense in applying it is vital, too.) Her business phone number is (617) 484-7432.

Clotilde
Box 22312
Ft. Lauderdale, FL 33335
G (contemporary); S
Catalogue: $1
Excellent source of the very best sewing supplies, books, videos.

Crazy Crow Trading Post
P.O. Box 314
Denison, TX 75020
G; P, S, R, A, M/W, B, O
Catalogue: $2
As the name suggests, they carry plenty of Indian items. However, you will want their pelts for Medieval wear, their tricorns, buttons, and more for Colonials, and other goodies for Civil War buffs.

Dazian
2014 Commerce Street
Dallas, TX 75201
G (contemporary); S
Catalogue: free
"The world's largest and oldest theatrical fabric organization" deals in contemporary supplies, but many can be used for reproduction wear. Their buckram hat frames are especially useful. Orders shipped in 24 hours.

Diana Venegas
8704 Sunset Blvd.
Los Angeles, CA 90069
G (V, E); R, C
Catalogue: none; Phone: (213) 659-6272
If you've always wanted one of those lacy, romantic gowns that you've seen on Hollywood stars, this is where you'll find them. Diana Venegas does not do business by mail, but her clothing is the ultimate in elegance. Her specialties are ballgowns and wedding gowns. She creates custom designs for many international celebrities.

Dorothy Bond
34706 Row River Road
Cottage Grove, OR 97424
G; B
Catalogue: Send long SASE for information
Author and publisher of *Embroidery Stitches from Old American Quilts* (see References), and other inspiring books.

Dover Publications, Inc.
31 East 2nd St.
Mineola, NY 11501
G; B
Catalogue: free
Dover publishes and reprints some of the most interesting historical books, at prices so low that I don't know how they can afford to stay in business. Excellent.

Dressing Screen/Jeanne M. Giroux
2 Manning Avenue
Troy, NY 12180
V, Ed, 20th; V
Wholesale vintage clothing, 1840–1940.

Eagle Feather Trading Post
706 W. Riverdale Rd.
Ogden, UT 84403
G, (C, F); P, S, R, A, M/W/C, B, O
Catalogue: $3, refundable with order
    Simple, well-constructed patterns; nice range of books and supplies. The men's breeches pattern fits perfectly to size.

Eileen McMillan
P.O. Box 674
Denver, NC 28037
V; R
Catalogue: send long SASE
    In addition to pillow shams, Eileen carries several Victorian clothing items.

Elsie's Exquisiques
205 Elizabeth Drive
Berrien Springs, MI 49103
G (contemporary); S
Catalogue: Send long SASE for information
    Spectacular array of trim for clothing, doll clothes, and so on.

Folkwear
Box 3859
San Rafael, CA 94912
G; P, M/W/C
Catalogue: Send SASE for information
    Although Folkwear patterns have been available in stores and through sources such as Amazon Dry Goods, you may want to write to the company directly. At press time, the company was undergoing management changes which may affect pattern availability.

Fruit of the Vine
4306 Sunset Drive
Los Angeles, CA 90027
M/R, V, G; C, A
Catalogue: SASE for information
    Fruit of the Vine makes accurate and spectacular costumes and historical garments, at prices that are sensible and affordable. Specializing in clothing with the right look, on a tight budget. One of the few costumers who specifically mentions washable costumes.

Gibson Lee, Inc.
78 Stone Place
Melrose, MA 02176
G (V, Ed); R, M
Catalogue: free brochure
  Reasonably priced disposable collars and cuffs (and the shirts for them) for costume use. Also spats, minister's collars. Volume purchases may be necessary; similar items in smaller volume are available from Amazon.

Gohn Brothers
Box 111
Middlebury, IN 45640
G (contemporary); R, M/W/C, O
Catalogue: long SASE for information
  An extraordinary company which carries "old-fashioned" clothing for the Amish and Mennonite communities, among others.

Good Impressions
The Old General Store
Shirley, WV 26434-0033
G (V); O
Catalogue: $2
  No clothing or patterns, but Good Impressions carries some wonderful rubber stamps I use frequently, featuring authentic Victorian designs. Once you're hooked on Victoriana, you'll want stamps, too.

Green River Forge, Ltd.
Box 257
Fulton, CA 95439
G (C, P, CW); P, S, R, A, M/W/C, B, O
Catalogue: $4
  Catalogue is unusually informative about clothing details. Company staff is very helpful, too.

Gutcheon Patchworks, Inc.
584 Broadway
New York, NY 10012
G (20th); S
Catalogue: $2, includes fabric swatches
  Sewing supplies, books, and some of the most hauntingly beautiful cotton fabrics. They're designed for quilters, but I find them to be some of the best color combinations and designs for Victorian clothing.

Harriet Engler
1930 W. Marne Avenue
Glendale, WI 53209
G (V, CW); P, S, R, C, A, M/W/C
Catalogue: $2

Patterns, accessories, and readymades, primarily for the Civil War years. She created many of the hats for the miniseries, "North and South."

Heidi Marsh
810 El Caminito
Livermore, CA 94550
V (CW); P, S, R
Catalogue: $1 for pattern catalogue

Some of the most wonderful, inexpensive patterns from the Hoop Era (Victorian, Civil War), for men, women and children. Heidi also has plates from magazines (catalogue, $5.50), and color plates suitable for framing (catalogue, $4.50).

Henson's Victorian Footwear & Accessories
P.O. Box 403
Kailua, HI 97634
V; F
Catalogue: long SASE for information

In the text, I mentioned an upcoming source of Victorian high-button boots. As of this writing, production of the boots is still under negotiation with manufacturers. If you're interested, I recommend that you write for more information, and get on the waiting list quickly.

Hooker-Howe Costume Co.
Box 98
Bradford, MA 01830
G; R, M/W/C, E
Catalogue: free brochure

Over 60,000 costume items in stock, including wigging, makeup, boots, shoes, and props.

House of York
32 N. Union St.
Elgin, IL 60120
V (CW); B
Catalogue: long SASE for information
 Author and publisher of *Civil War Sketchbooks*, Volumes I, II, and III (see References). Vital for women's Civil War costuming.

Irish Ventures
P.O. Box 426
New York, NY 10024
V; S
Catalogue: free
 The only outlet in America for new Carrickmacross lace, a Victorian-era lace. Each piece is entirely handmade in Ireland. Surprisingly affordable.

Joseph's Coat
26 Main Street
Peterborough, NH 03458
G (20th); S, P, B
Catalogue: Send SASE
 If you live anywhere in New England, it is worth the drive to this little shop, for the exquisite fabrics, goodies, and creative ideas. Their classes are excellent, too. For those too distant to visit the shop, send for a catalogue of the latest sewing delights.

Joslin Hall Books
P.O. Box 516
Concord, MA 01742
B
Catalogue: free
 Contemporary books about art and antiques, including costume, fashion, and needlework. Rare and out-of-print books on the decorative arts, including textiles, fashions, lace, and tapestry. Customers' special interests kept on file.

June K. Garges
1125 Sparrow Road
Audubon, PA 19403
G; B
Catalogue: long SASE for information
Author and publisher of *Handcrafted Straw Hats* (see References).

Kathleen B. Smith
Box 48
West Chesterfield, MA 01084
C; S
Catalogue: $1
The most magnificent, authentic materials for creating 18th-century clothing. You must get her catalogue if you are working on Colonial clothing. Excellent quality and surprisingly low prices.

Lace Broker, The
252 Newbury Street
Boston, MA 02116
G; R
Catalogue: none; phone (617) 267-5954
Wholesale and retail vintage and antique textiles. Specializes in lace.

Lacis
2990 Adeline Street
Berkeley, CA 94703
G; V, P, S, B, O
Catalogue: $1, tools, books, supplies
Specializing in antique and vintage lace and costume, conservation materials, books and patterns. Source for stays, corset supplies, antique trim and buttons. Conservation and restoration services, too. Acid-free tissue paper and acid-free boxes for safely storing your treasures.

The Ladies Companion
P.O. Box 31152
St. Louis, MO 63131
V, CW; R, C, A, W/C, B, O, E
Catalogue: $2
This delightful company offers absolutely wonderful clothes and accessories at affordable prices. Over 100 items from wedding gowns to undergarments, hats to stockings.

Linda White
100 Main Street
Upton, MA 01587
G (V); V
No catalogue
Send a list of what you need. Especially knowledgeable about parasols.

Linen & Lace
337 St. Mary St.
Lewisburg, PA 17837
G (V, Ed); V, R, C
Catalogue: $3
Owner Linda Doebler makes magnificent reproduction clothing, as well as buying and selling vintage and antique clothing. Her reproduction clothing is some of the best available, and she specializes in Victorian and Edwardian reproductions, wholesale and retail.

Log Cabin Shop, The
P.O. Box 275
Lodi, OH 44254
G (C, Ft, V); P, R, A, M/W/C, B, O, G, E
Catalogue: $4
Thick catalogue of historical items.

Magico Magazine
P.O. Box 156
New York, NY 10002-0156
V; B, O
Catalogue: $1
Nothing to do with clothing per se, but if you're going to get involved with Sherlock Holmes' era and groups, you'll want this catalogue of the latest Holmes books and related items.

Marybeth Buchele
20845 Radisson Inn Road
Exelsior, MN 55331
G; O
Catalogue: SASE for information; $1 for sweater mailer and info
Sweaters repaired to look like new. This is not "invisible weaving," which is rarely invisible!

Medieval Miscellanea
700 Raleigh Road
Annandale, VA 22003
M/R; P, S, R, A, M/W, B, J, F, O, G
Catalogue: $1
Delightful catalogue of Medieval and Renaissance items.

Mini-Magic Carpet
3675 Reed Road
Columbus, OH 43220
G (contemporary); S, O
Catalogue: long SASE for information
Unusual list of items, including decorative trim, conservation supplies, and more.

Nancy's Notions
P.O. Box 683
Beaver Dam, WI 53916
G; S
Fun sewing goodies (and plenty of essentials) that will make sewing easier and make your garments look more professional.

New Columbia
P.O. Box 524
Charleston, IL 61920
G (19th, 20th); R, C, A, M/W
Catalogue: $2
Readymade 19th-century clothing for men and women, and a separate catalogue of WWI and WWII uniforms and accessories.

Old Chatham Clothing Company
Old Chatham, NY 12136
G (20th); V, M/W
Catalogue: $1
Wild vintage clothing featured in a photo-illustrated catalogue. Mostly 20th century, some earlier.

Old Fort Hill Mercantile
102 East Somonauk
Yorkville, IL 60560
C, Ft, Re, V; R, C, M/W/C, O, B, E
Catalogue: $2

Historically accurate reproductions of clothing from 1750–1850. Also muzzle-loading supplies, books, and more. This company is managed by delightful people with a sincere interest in practical but authentic costuming.

Old World Sewing Pattern Company
Rt. 2, Box 103
Cold Spring, MN 56320
Re, V; P, M/W
Catalogue: $1

Classic designs from several years. Discount prices for large orders.

Ouabache Press
P.O. Box 2076
West Lafayette, IN 47906
C; B
Catalogue: long SASE for information

Publishers of *Historic Colonial French Dress*, one of the best resources for Colonial clothing.

Past Patterns
2017 Eastern S.E.
Grand Rapids, MI 49507
V, Ed, 20th; P, S, R, M/W/C, B
Catalogue: $5 for Victorian/Edwardian catalogue; or ask for free brochure

The ultimate patterns for accurate and elegant clothing of the past. The owner is especially helpful and knowledgeable. Authentic designs have been proportioned to comfortably fit modern women.

Patience & Purity Pattern Co.
P.O. Box 476
Goffstown, NH 03045
V, Ed; P
Catalogue: $1 for brochure

Wonderful patterns based on historical fashions. Whimsical and romantic styles.

Patterns of History
816 State Street
Madison, WI 53706
V; P, M/W, C
Catalogue: send long SASE
    Each major Victorian period is represented. Pattern enclosures describe fashion era in detail, and are invaluable.

Pegee of Williamsburg
P.O. Box 127
Williamsburg, VA 23187-0127
C, Re, CW; P, M/W
Catalogue: send long SASE
    Some of the best, easiest patterns for Colonial times. Other eras, too. Highly recommended.

Pieces of Dreams
32275 St. Vincent
Warren, MI 48092
G (V, Ed, 20th); R, C, M/W/C, O
Catalogue: long SASE for brochure
    Custom reproductions of antique clothing, geared especially to classic car collectors. Wedding fashions and others also available. Emphasis on authenticity and customer satisfaction.

Products of the Past
West Main Street
Wilmington, VT 05363
C; P, R, A, M/W/C, O
Catalogue: $2
    Unusual items and familiar merchandise.

Promenade's Le Bead Shop
P.O. Box 2092
Boulder, CO 80306
G (contemporary); S, B
Catalogue: $2.50
    Beads, beadwork supplies, kits, instructions books, and more.

Quilting Books Unlimited
156 S. Gladstone
Aurora, IL 60506
G (20th); B
Catalogue: $1

If you're thinking of creating clothing that includes pieced, appliquéd, or patchwork designs, this is the source for inspiring books. They carry every quilting book currently in print, and they're nice people, too.

R. L. Shep
Box C-20
Lopez Island, WA 98261
B
Catalogue: $2.50 for rare books catalogue

R. L. Shep regularly reprints books related to period clothing. Send a SASE for their current list. They also publish a catalogue of rare, out-of-print books.

Raymond's Quiet Press
P.O. Box 35118
Albuquerque, NM 87176
M/R; A, J, O
Catalogue: send long SASE

One of the best sources for Medieval and Renaissance Jewelry, books, and other very special items. Nice people, too.

Recollections
3340 Avon, #446
Hartland, MI 48029
V, Ed; R, C, W
Catalogue: $2

Exquisite, carefully made reproductions of Victorian and Edwardian clothing. Wholesale and retail.

Rideable Bicycle Replicas
2447 Telegraph Avenue
Oakland, CA 94612
19th; O
Write for information

Top-quality reproductions of bicycles of the past. Very fancy.

Sew Craft
Box 1869
Warsaw, IN 46580
G (contemporary); S
Catalogue: $1.50 (or $5 for 4 quarterly issues)
Unique sewing supplies, books, and inspiring advice in a newspaper-format catalogue.

Shaeffer, Claire
P.O. Box 157-B
Palm Springs, CA 92263
G (20th); B
If your bookstore doesn't have Claire's *Complete Book of Sewing Shortcuts*, you can contact her directly for this superb book. (See description in References)

Silver Thread Creations
c/o V. Long
1317 N. Choctaw
Dewey, OK 74029
G; R, C, A, M/W/C
Catalogue: $5, applied toward first purchase
Readymade and custom-made clothing at affordable prices. Covers most eras. Authentic copies of clothing from 1700–1955.

Stitch In Time, A
832 Glengary
Toledo, OH 43617
G; R, C, W/C
Catalogue: $1
Custom-made period clothing, women's and children's outerwear and underpinnings. Some antique items, too. High quality, low prices.

Sutler of Mount Misery
G. Gedney Godwin
Box 100
Valley Forge, PA 19481
C, Ft, CW; R, C, M/W/C, B, O, F, E
Catalogue: $3.50 for enormous price list with illustrations
These folks are to Colonials what Amazon Dry Goods is to Victorians. In other words, this sutler carries everything you'll need, and then some.

Textile Home Companion/Maiden in the Meadow
5606 State Rt. 37
Delaware, OH 43015
G, (18th, 19th); S, R, O
Catalogue: THC, $3; Maiden, $2
These two separate lines from the same company feature many fabrics and readymade items of interest to 18th and early 19th-century costumers. The authentic homespun textiles are especially unique and colorful, while remaining accurate for historical use.

Thai Silks
252 State Street
Los Altos, CA 94022
G (contemporary); S
Catalogue: free
A wide range of affordable silks for all eras. Their raw silks are especially nice.

The Wish Booklets
Susan Sirkis
11909 Blue Spruce Road
Reston, VA 22091
G (contemporary); S, B
Catalogue: long SASE for information
Publisher of excellent series of booklets on fabric arts.

Theodore F. Monnich
P.O. Box 13292
Memphis, TN 38113-0292
M/R; O
Catalogue: $1
Design, reproduction, conservation, and restoration of arms and armour, bronze, silver, and iron antiquities. Armour reproductions of 14th through 17th centuries.

Treadleart
25834-1 Narbonne Ave.
Lomita, CA 90717
G (20th); S
Superb supplies for fun sewing.

Tumbleweed
99 Mt. Auburn St.
Cambridge, MA 02138
G (20th); S
Catalogue: $1.75, includes fabric swatches
A wonderful store in Harvard Square, with knowledgeable sales-people to help you find the right fabrics for your needs. Great calicoes for Victorian clothing. They have prompt service by mail, too.

Vermont Country Store
P.O. Box 3000
Manchester, VT 05255-3000
G (contemporary); S, R, A, M/W, O
A classic catalogue of common-sense items, many of which have been around since the 19th century. Their natural herb moth repel-lents are excellent for storing vintage clothing. One of my favorite mail-order catalogues, even before I became interested in costuming.

Vintage Connection, The
P.O. Box 4543
Montgomery, AL 36101
V, Ed; V, A, W
Catalogue: $3 for an illustrated, beautiful catalogue
Generally below-wholesale prices on one-of-a-kind items from the Edwardian era. Some Victorian, 1920s, etc.

Vintage Reproductions
Sharon Clark
514 North First Street
Bismarck, ND 58501
G (V, Ed); R, C
Sews reproductions of vintage clothing. Very knowledgeable.

Washington Millinery Supply, Inc.
P.O. Box 5718
Derwood, MD 20855
G (contemporary); S
Catalogue: $5 retail; free with business name and license number
Supplies for making hats. Some are suitable for reproductions.

Wichelt Imports
Rural Route #1
Stoddard, WI 54658
G (contemporary); S
This company carries quality fabrics for reproductions. One of their fabrics is Shannon Cloth, a linen and cotton blend similar to fustian.

With Needle and Thread
Judith Foster
601 San Pable Avenue, #J
Rodeo, CA 94572
G; R, C, M/W/C
Catalogue: Large SASE and $1
Designs and sews period clothing, not costumes, to fit the modern body.

Wonderful World of Hats
209 N.E. Harney Street
Newport, OR 97365
G; P, S, C, A, M/W/C, B, O
Catalogue: $3
One of the best sources for information and supplies for making hats. They have mail-order courses, too. Will do custom work. Great books.

Wooden Porch Books
Rt. 1, Box 262
Middlebourne, WV 26149
B
Catalogue: $2 for next 3 issues
Excellent prices and fast service on out-of-print books, magazines, and other goodies related to fashion, costume, needlework, and textiles.

Clubs, Organizations, Periodicals

This section lists major clubs and organizations for people interested in historical fashions. It also includes magazines and newsletters related to clothing and costuming. There is a brief list of the major sponsors of vintage clothing shows and other events. By keeping in touch with these people, you'll be kept up-to-date on your favorite aspects of historical clothing, and find opportunities to share your interests with others.

Many of these groups are non-profit. When writing for information, please include a long, self-addressed stamped envelope (SASE), and mention *Sewing and Collecting Vintage Fashions.*

CLUBS AND ORGANIZATIONS

Thousands of groups are involved in the many areas related to history and historical clothing. Following are some of the largest and most popular for specific costuming interests. Through these groups, you will learn about other organizations.

Adventuresses of Sherlock Holmes, The
c/o Ms. Evelyn Herzog
235 W. 15th Street
New York, NY 10011
    One of the few Sherlock Holmes groups for women. Send a long SASE to receive their next (infrequent but excellent) mailing.

American Association for State and Local History
172 Second Avenue North, Suite 102
Nashville, TN 37201
    Variety of publications and services for individuals and groups involved in preserving history.

Baker Street Irregulars
c/o Julian Wolff
33 Riverside Dr.
New York, NY 10023

Loosely organized literary society devoted to the study of Sherlock Holmes. Main activities include a horse race at the Belmont each year, and an annual dinner in January.

Bye Gone Eras
The Bonners
5308 Leader Avenue
Sacramento, CA 95841

Group of people who love to recreate the history of times past through extensive research and theatrical presentation. Most events are in Northern California. Send long SASE for information.

Costume Society of America
P.O. Box 73
Earleville, MD 21919

Dark Shadows Fan Club of Southern California, The
P.O. Box 69A04
West Hollywood, CA 90069

Club for fans of the Victorian-costumed soap opera, "Dark Shadows." Regular events, cast reunions, etc.

Friends of Dark Shadows
P.O. Box 213
Metairie, LA 70004

National organization devoted to "Dark Shadows." Costuming is from 18th and 19th centuries. Sample issue of Journal, $4.

Friends of the English Regency
c/o Elaine Pelz
15931 Kalisher St.
Granada Hills, CA 91344

Loosely knit group of people interested in different facets of the Regency, including costuming and dance. Sample newsletter, $1.

International Club for Collectors of Hatpins & Hatpin Holders
15237 Chanera Avenue
Gardena, CA 90249

The name says it all. Send them a long SASE for information.

Jane Austen Society of North America
c/o Joan Brantz
P.O. Box 28744
Elkins Park, PA 19117

Organization for the study and enjoyment of Jane Austen's life and works. Send a long, double-stamped, self-addressed envelope for information about this enthusiastic group.

Living History Association
P.O. Box 578
Wilmington, VT 05363

Large organization of reenactors, with a primary focus on Colonial times. Send $1 for information packet.

North-South Skirmish Association
9700 Royerton Drive
Richmond, VA 23228

Provides competition with Civil War firearms, but also includes reenactments of camp life at many events. One of the oldest of the living history organizations.

Society for Creative Anachronism — SCA Registry
P.O. Box 360743
Milpitas, CA 95035

Recreates garb, culture and technology of the European Middle Ages and Renaissance. Over 500 branches in the U.S. and abroad.

Somewhere In Time, Unlimited
c/o Nelle Goldade
3409 172nd SW
Lynwood, WA 98037

Recreates Victorian balls, 1920s speakeasies, other past-time entertainment in the greater Seattle area. Period dress must be worn. $1 plus SASE for mailing.

Textile Society of America
c/o Peg Gilfoy
Indianapolis Museum of Art
1200 West 38th St.
Indianapolis, IN 46208

United States Institute for Theatre Technicians
330 West 42nd Street, Suite 1702
New York, NY 10036
   Fabulous organization for costumers and others involved in theater. Regional and national activities. Call or write for membership information. (212) 563-5551.

Victorian Society, The
E. Washington Square
Philadelphia, PA 19106
   National organization with local chapters. Regular publications, local and national events, all related to the Victorian era.

PERIODICALS

These are a few of the best publications for people interested in historical fashions. Some are very small and have a specific audience, while others are quite general and readily available.

Aardvark Territorial Enterprise
P.O. Box 2449
Livermore, CA 94550
   Although this is actually a mail-order catalogue (see Resources), it is also one of the most delightful publications related to fabric art. $1 for sample copy; you'll read it cover to cover.

Antique Jewelry Letter
P.O. Box 620
Bedford, Nova Scotia, Canada B4A 3H4
   Bimonthly educational newsletter for antique jewelry novices and experts. Sample issue, $3.

Baker Street Gazette
Baker Street Publications
P.O. Box 994
Metairie, LA 70004
   Quarterly publication devoted to Sherlock Holmes and Victorian times. Sample copy, $3.

Bias Line
115 South Manhattan
Tampa, FL 33609
  Fascinating newsletter for costumers and theater technicians. Especially good for people involved in small theaters who need to know where to find supplies. $2 for sample issue.

Fiberarts
Nine Press
50 College Street
Asheville, NC 28801
  Look for this magazine at your bookstore or fabric shop, or write for subscription rates. Not a historical publication, not limited to clothing, but has excellent sources and innovative ideas.

Fiction Writers Magazine
Romantic Times Publications
163 Joralemon St.
Brooklyn Heights, NY 11201
  Articles, sources, and research tips. Although published for writers, articles often describe clothing and manners of the past; as interesting to history buffs as it is to authors.

Hayes Historical Journal
Hayes Presidential Center
Spiegel Grove
Fremont, OH 43420
  A quarterly publication about The Gilded Age, during the Presidency of Rutherford B. Hayes.

Molly's/Grandmother's Vintage Gazette
P.O. Box 191
Maynard, MA 01754
  Quarterly newsletter devoted to the vintage clothing business scene. Articles on shows, auctions, exhibits, books, and news. $6 per year.

Ornament
P.O. Box 35029
Los Angeles, CA 90035
  A spectacular magazine, not limited to clothing, full of ideas for ornamentation of all kinds. Very innovative approaches, as well as traditional styles.

Regency Network
c/o Nora Siri Bock
CBS News, Cronkite Unit
555 West 57th St.
New York, NY 10019
   An information exchange among writers and readers interested in the Regency period. Subscription, $5.

Romantic Times Magazine
163 Joralemon St.
Brooklyn Heights, NY 11201
   Articles, reviews, and interesting information related to romance novels. Since many of them are historical romances, you'll find information about your favorite eras, too.

Stumpwork Society Chronicle
P.O. Box 122
Bogota, NJ 07603
   The newsletter of the Stumpwork Society, which documents decorative embroidery techniques. Patterns, samples, illustrations fill this informative newsletter. $10 per year.

Threads
The Taunton Press
63 South Main St.
Newtown, CT 06470
   A fairly mainstream magazine for fiber artists, with many creative ideas for clothing and accessories. Look for it in most bookstores.

EVENTS

Bellow Canto
4306 Sunset Drive
Los Angeles, CA 90027
   A musical group which provides period vocals to accompany historical events. These people have great costumes and a terrific sense of humor. (213) 663-1669.

Joan Caddigan
P.O. Box 497
Norwell, MA 02061

Specialty auctions, including vintage clothing. Write to Mrs. Caddigan about her Auctions-by-Mail of clothing and accessories.

High Moon Productions
P.O. Box 313
Hull, MA 02045

Dress in costume and live your fantasies with this troupe of actors who present audience-participation adventures, including "Murder With A Twist." Send SASE for upcoming schedule.

Jeffrey Kurash
P.O. Box 177
Lowell, FL 32663

Sponsors major vintage clothing shows in the Southeast, especially Florida. Send long SASE for information.

Molly's/Grandmother's Promotions
P.O. Box 191
Maynard, MA 01754

Some of the world's largest vintage clothing shows, presented in Auburn, Mass. every May and September. Send long SASE for discount cards and further information.

References

Many valuable books about historical clothing and the times when they were worn are listed in this section. Many are available through regular bookstores, while others can be ordered from historical suppliers, such as Amazon Dry Goods, Eagle Feather, Green River Forge, and Past Patterns, all of which are listed in Resources. In some cases, you may have to write directly to the publisher, or find out-of-print books from rare book dealers, such as R. L. Shep, Wooden Porch, Joslin Hall, and Bette Feinstein, also listed in Resources.

I have described many of the books, some of which are in my personal reference collection. Others, without description, have been enthusiastically endorsed by historical clothing professionals. Remember when you're at auctions or used book stores to watch for self-published "Sketchbooks." You can usually rely on them to be helpful and inexpensive costume references for "your" era.

1896 Illustrated Catalogue of Jewelry & Fashions. Marshall Field & Co. (1970, Gun Digest, paperback).

> Extensive, illustrated volume of items made of silver, including tableware, accessories, and jewelry. Small fashion section at the back.

1897 Sears, Roebuck Catalogue. (Reprinted 1976, Chelsea House, paperback).

America's Printed and Painted Fabrics. Pettit, Florence H. (1970, Hastings House).

American Historical Supply Catalogue. Wellikoff, Alan (1984, Schocken Books, paperback).

> Delightful list of sources of newly manufactured items from the past. Includes clothing, housewares, toys, food, musical instruments, building supplies, military goods, frontier items, pipes and tobacco, and more.

An Edwardian Summer. Goodall, John S. (1976, Atheneum, hardcover).

  Watercolor pictures of the everyday events in an English village during the early 1900s. All of Goodall's books give a wonderful feeling for the eras they represent.

The Anatomy of Costume. Selbie and Ambrus (1982).

  Stylized, colorful illustrations, with descriptions of fashions from antiquity to the 1960s.

Antique Children's Fashions, 1880–1900: A Handbook for Doll Costumers. Ulseth & Shannon (1982, Hobby House Press, paperback).

  Well-illustrated study of children's clothing of the era, with sewing tips that can be used on full-size clothing as well as for dolls. Some patterns.

Antique Fashion Paper Dolls for the 1890's. Boston Children's Museum (1984, Dover Press, paperback, $3.50).

  Two paper dolls and thirty costumes that originally appeared in The Boston *Herald* Sunday newspaper, 1895–96. Delightful.

Authentic Costuming for Historic Site Guides. Severa, Joan (1979, AASLH, Technical Leaflet 113).

  Remarkably extensive guide to creating accurate historical costumes. Order directly from American Assn. for State and Local History (see Resources listing for address).

Bags and Purses. Foster, Vanda (1982, Batsford, hardcover).

  One of several excellent reference books in Batsford's Costume Accessory Series. Other titles include *Hats* and *Gloves.*

The Book of Costume, or Annals of Fashion (1846) by A Lady of Rank. The Countess of Wilton and R. L. Shep (reprinted 1987, R. L. Shep, $45.00 + $2.50 postage).

  Described as a detailed history of costume and fashion in England and France from earliest times to 1800. Also includes folk dress. Order directly from the publisher (see Resources).

Calico Chronicle: Texas Women and Their Fashions, 1830–1910. Mills, Betty J. Savage (1985, Texas Tech Press, $25.95).

  Valuable details and illustrations for the early years in Texas. Excellent reference for general Victorian use, too.

Children's Costume in America, 1607–1910. Worrell, Estelle Ansley (1980, Scribner's, hardcover).

  Illustrations and detailed descriptions of children's historical clothing.

Civil War Ladies Sketchbook: Volumes 1, 2 and 3. York, K. A. (1980, House of York, paperback.

  Wonderful details and fresh costuming ideas. Some patterns. Vital for women's Civil War era clothing.

ClothesCare: Secrets of the Professionals. Wagenvoord and St. Aubyn (1985, Wallaby Books, paperback, $6.95).

Cleaning, care and storage information. Contains stain removal chart. One of the many excellent books on this topic.

Clothing Guidelines for the Civil War Era. Burgess, Janet (1985, Amazon Dry Goods, paperback, $5 postpaid).

An essential guide for men's and women's Victorian costuming, especially for the Civil War. Included is the vital "Amazon Theory of Hoop Relativity," to create a skirt in the correct size. (See Resources for address).

Collectible Clothing with Prices. Malouff, Sheila (1987, Wallace-Homestead, paperback).

A new book featuring photographs and prices. Books like these are fun to read, but prices vary widely from one area to another, and photos don't always show quality. With these factors in mind, the photos will give you many ideas of items you might want to find or recreate.

Collecting Costume: The Care and Display of Clothes and Accessories. Tarrant, Naomi (1983, Allen & Unwin, hardcover).

Detailed text on what is available, building your collection, storage, repair, display, and more. Vital reading for collectors.

A Colorful Book. Porcella, Yvonne (1986, Porcella Studios, paperback, $22).

If you're hesitant about combining colors and color wheels leave you cold, this is the reference book to help you select the color families you want in your wardrobe. (To order, see Porcella Studios in Resources.)

The Complete Book of Machine Embroidery. Fanning, Robbie and Tony (1986, Chilton, $16.95).

One of the best books on using your sewing machine, Far more than just embroidery. Vital information on needles, threads, and so on.

The Complete Book of Sewing Shortcuts. Shaeffer, Claire B. (1981, Sterling Publishing, hardcover; 1982, paperback).

Sewing basics and shortcuts to make your clothing as much fun to sew (well, almost) as it is to wear. Clearly illustrated, with simple, detailed instructions for those of us who are "all thumbs" when it comes to tailoring.

Corsets and Crinolines. Waugh, Norah (1981, Theatre Arts Books).

Costume 1066–1966. Peacock, John (1986, Thames & Hudson, paperback).

One of the most useful illustrated references for all eras.

Costume in Detail. Bradfield, Nancy.

> Careful illustrations of garments from 1730 through 1930. Some garments are the same as those in Janet Arnold's *Patterns of History*, so the volumes work well together when you are constructing one of the patterns.

Costume in England: A History of Dress to the End of the 18th Century. Fairholt, F. W., enlarged by Dillon, H. A. (1885, reissued 1968).

> Illustrated guide to English fashions. Excellent material on detailing for pre-1066 clothing, too.

Costumer's Handbook: How to make all kinds of costumes. Ingham and Covey (1980, Prentice-Hall, paperback.

> Reliable ideas for creating stage-quality costumes.

Costumes of Everyday Life. Lister, Margot (1972).

> An excellent costume reference for the years 900–1910. The black and white line drawings and descriptions cover everyday wear and clothing worn for specific kinds of work.

Costumes Through the Ages. Braun, et al. (1981, Rizzoli International).

> Color plates and descriptions of costumes from antiquity through the 19th century. Especially good for regional costumes of Europe and Asia.

Decorative Dressmaking. Thompson, Sue (1985, Rodale Press, hardcover).

> Delightful ideas for creative clothing, packed with tips, instructions and colorful illustrations. A clever book that will inspire you, no matter what your sewing interests.

Dictionary of Costume. Wilcox, R. Turner.

> Heavily illustrated reference book in dictionary form, covering over 3,200 words related to costume.

Distaff Sketch Book. Klinger (Pioneer Press, paperback).

> Valuable sketches and patterns for women's clothing of the American Revolution.

Dress and Cloak Cutter: Women's Costume, 1877–1882. Hecklinger, Charles (expanded from original text, 1987; R. L. Shep, paperback, $15.95 + $1.05 postage).

> An expanded version of an 1881 book, it includes the princess style dress and a large variety of outerwear. Illustrated, with patterns. Order direct from the publisher (see Resources).

Early American Dress. Warwick, Pitz, and Wyckoff (1965, Benjamin Blom, hardcover).

> Illustrated textbook detailing men's, women's and children's clothing of the first two centuries in America.

Embroidery Stitches from Old American Quilts. Bond, Dorothy (1977, Dorothy Bond, paperback).

Fantastic illustrations of fancy embroidery, to add a special touch to your clothing and accessories. A favorite book.

Encyclopedia of Fashion. O'Hara, Georgina (1986, Abrams, hardcover).

Illustrated, dictionary-style text covering terms and names from historical and contemporary fashion eras.

Evolution of Fashion: Pattern and Cut from 1066 to 1930. Hill and Bucknell (first published 1967, Batsford, hardcover).

Descriptions, illustrations, and simple patterns for each major fashion era.

Fabric of Society, 1770–1870. Tozer and Levitt (1983, Laura Ashley, hardcover).

Photos, illustrations, and descriptions of clothing and fabrics of this period. Invaluable.

Five Ethnic Patterns. Porcella, Yvonne.

Basic patterns that can be adapted for a vintage look. Ideal for sewing garments of vintage fabrics, with a minimum of cutting.

Garb of Country New Englanders, 1790–1840. Fennelly, Catherine (1966, Old Sturbridge Village, paperback).

Photos and descriptions of clothing, mostly women's, from the post-Revolutionary period.

Great Fashion Designs of the Belle Epoque. Tierney, Tom (1982, Dover Books, paperback, $3.50).

Paper dolls showing the most dazzling gowns from the best designers of this era. Magnificent and inspiring.

Handbook of Practical Cutting on the Centre Point System (1866). Devere, Louis (1986, R. L. Shep, paperbound, $17.95 + $1.05 p&h).

A reprint of an 1866 book, described as "Tailoring men's garments. . .1850's, 1860's, 1870's. ." Order directly from the publisher, R. L. Shep (see Resources).

Handcrafted Straw Hats. Garges, June Kraft (1982, June K. Garges, paperback).

How-to guide to making authentic straw hats.

Hat Lovers' Dictionary. (1985, Wonderful World of Hats, paperback).

Words and illustrations to guide you to the correct hats for your era. Includes descriptions of items used to create hats, such as different types of veiling.

Heirloom Sewing. Pierce, Margaret (1981, Margaret Pierce).

One of the many excellent books you'll find in specialty sewing shops. This one features the finishing techniques which will make your Victorian and Edwardian clothing spectacular. Vital for creating dazzling tea gowns.

Historic Colonial French Dress. Johnson, Forbes, and Delaney (1982, Ouabache Press, paperback).

One of the best guides to recreating Colonial clothing. Descriptions, background, patterns, illustrations, and delightful trivia. Useful for non-French Colonial costuming, too.

Historic Costume for the Stage. Barton, Lucy (1935).

Costuming ideas, and details that can be used for accuracy or simplified for an authentic touch to a "quick costume." The text covers antiquity through 1914, and there are some drawings. Writers will appreciate the era-by-era descriptions with historic references to put the eras in a more familiar context.

Historic Dress of the Old West. Reedstrom, Ernest Lisle (1986, Blandford, hardcover, $19.95).

Illustrations and descriptions of men's and women's clothing in western America during the 19th century. Some children's clothing, and Plains Indian clothing. Excellent background data.

History of Children's Costume. Ewing, Elizabeth (1977).

A well-illustrated text which covers the 15th century to the present day.

A History of Costume. Kohler and von Sichart (1928; slightly different from the later Dover reproduction).

Well-illustrated text which includes some patterns for eras back to ancient Egypt.

A History of Make-Up. Angeloglou, Maggie (1970).

Living history participants and writers will be delighted with this illustrated book that covers antiquity through the 1960s. It covers cosmetics, perfume, and all aspects of make-up.

History of Underclothes. Willett and Cunnington (revised by Mansfields).

Detailed documentary of underclothes throughout history.

How to Make Sad Old Hats Sparkle Anew. (1985, Wonderful World of Hats, paperback).

If you're buying wearables, this book is worth its weight in gold. It is actually a course that takes you through each step of making an old, damaged, dirt-covered hat into something wearable. Some hat patterns, too.

The Illustrated Encyclopedia of Costume and Fashion 1550–1920. Cassin-Scott, Jack (1971).

Very stylized color illustrations that are a good overview when trying to determine the years of a style that you have in mind.

It's You! Cho, Emily (1986, Ballantine, paperback, $7.95).

The Arty and Romantic sections of this book will give you ideas for including historical clothing in your everyday wardrobe.

Ladies' Guide to Needlework. Frost, S. Annie (1986, R. L. Shep, paperback, $9.95 + $1.05 p&h).

Patterns and illustrations for hundreds of projects, including embroidery, knitting, tatting, bead work, and appliqué. Many Victorian clothing and accessory items. Order direct from publisher (see Resources) Ideal for historical clothing buffs.

Linens and Old Lace. Martin and Saltkill (That Patchwork Place, paperback).

Illustrations and patterns for including antique textiles in your clothing and household items. Great ideas and suggestions.

Living History Sourcebook. Anderson, Jay (1985, AASLH, paperback).

Invaluable guide to sites, organizations, suppliers, and more. Can be ordered from American Association for State and Local History (see Resources).

Mr. Godey's Ladies. Kunciov, Robert, editor (1971).

A brief overview of the Godey years (1830s through 1870s). It's only slightly more detailed than Heidi Marsh's mail-order catalogues, but the chronology at the opening of the book is a nice reference for writers.

The Mode in Costume. Wilcox, R. Turner (1958).

Descriptive text and line drawings cover antiquity through the 1950s. This is an outstanding costume reference book, highly recommended for use by writers. The text includes many fascinating details.

Needlework: An Historical Survey. Ring, Betty (Main Street Press, paperback).

Compilation of articles from "The Magazine Antiques," on the subject of needlework. Only one chapter specifically on clothing, but filled with important information for collectors and for anyone who wants precise details about needlework techniques of a particular era.

Patterns of Fashion 1, 1660–1860. Arnold, Janet (1964, Macmillan/Drama Books, paperback).

Detailed descriptions, drawings, and patterns. Unique because it shows the inside of the garments, including sewing details.

Patterns of Fashion 2, 1860–1940. Arnold, Janet.

Like her earlier book, Ms. Arnold includes detailed descriptions, patterns, and illustrations of original garments to the Victoria and Albert Museum. Several items from each era.

Pieced Clothing Variations. Porcella, Yvonne.

> Yvonne Porcella's books include basic patterns, many of which are historical, ethnic patterns. They can be used to include old and antique textiles and sewing techniques, to give your modern-day wardrobe an historical touch. (See Porcella Studios in Resources for address.)

Quilts in America. Orlofsky, Patsy and Myron (1974, McGraw-Hill, hardcover).

> Information on determining the age of fabrics and textiles. This out-of-print book sells for about $50 from used and rare book dealers, when you can find it. Check with your public library for a copy.

Riding Habits of the Era of the Hoop. Marsh, Heidi (1987, Heidi Marsh, paperback, $4.00 + $1.50 p&h).

> This well-illustrated booklet is filled with details about riding, 1857–1865. Excellent for living history. Order direct from publisher (see Resources).

Rural Pennsylvania Clothing. Gehret, Ellen J. (1976, Liberty Cap Press, hardcover).

> Absolutely wonderful book, due back in print in 1989. Over 300 readable pages of text and illustrations, covering everyday rural clothing, especially between 1750 and 1820. (See Liberty Cap Press in Resources list for address.)

Sketchbook '76. Klinger and Wilder, 1967, Pioneer Press, paperback).

> Superb basic guide to men's clothing during the American Revolution. Patterns, sketches and notes. (See Pioneer Press listing in Resources.)

Stumpwork Technique Suggestion. Fishman, Sylvia C. (1985, Sylvia C. Fishman, paperback).

> Stumpwork is a raised embroidery technique that reached its peak in the mid 17th century. This book gives historical and contemporary clothing suggestions for including stumpwork in your wardrobe. Also good for Victorian clothing. Patterns and illustrations included. Order from Stumpwork Society (see Resources).

Textile, Costume, and Doll Collections in the US and Canada. Bach, Pieter (1981, R. L. Shep, paperback, $4.95).

> A no-nonsense directory arranged geographically to guide you to the best collections. If your library doesn't have a copy, order directly from the publisher (see Resources).

Textiles in America, 1650–1870. Montgomery, Florence M. (Norton & Co., hardcover).

> Dictionary of textiles and related terms. Color photos are especially valuable when selecting fabrics for Colonial clothing.

The Textile Tools of Colonial Homes. Channing, Marion L. (1982, Channing Books, paperback).

If you're outfitting an authentic sewing room, filling an historically accurate sewing kit, or simply want to know what was used to create these wonderful fabrics and garments, this is a nice overview.

The Whole Costumer's Catalogue. (Published annually since 1982.)

Lists over 500 companies, in the U.S. and Canada, related to costuming.

The Wish Booklet, Volume XXIV. Sirkis, Susan (1983, Susan B. Sirkis, paperback).

Well-illustrated directions for using ribbon and lace as decorations on your clothing and accessories.

The Yestermorrow Clothes Book: How to Remodel Secondhand Clothes. Funaro, Diana (1976, Chilton Books, paperback).

Well-illustrated guide, filled with ideas for those treasures you'll find at the secondhand clothes store.

Two Centuries of Costume in America, 1620–1820. Earle, Alice Morse (1903, reissued in 1968).

Nicely illustrated reference book for early American clothing.

Victorian and Edwardian Fashion: A Photographic Survey. Gernsheim, Alison (1963, Dover Press, paperback, $6).

One of the most valuable reference books for Victorian clothing. Shows what men and women really wore. Excellent descriptions and 235 illustrations.

Victorian Costuming, Volume I: 1840 to 1865. Winter and Schultz.

Practical Victorian dressing for men, women, and children. Well illustrated, and contains valuable sewing tips.

Victorian Fashions & Costumes from Harper's Bazaar 1867–1898. Blum, Stella (1974, Dover Press, paperback, $9.95).

Enormous book, lavishly illustrated with detailed drawings showing high fashion for 1867–1898.

Victorians Abroad. Goodall, John S. (1981, Atheneum, hardcover).

Watercolors of typical travel scenes from the Victorian era, showing fashions, interiors, and the style of that time. Marvelous.

Visual History of Costume: The Eighteenth Century. Ribeiro, Aileen (Drama Books, hardcover).

This is one of several books in an excellent series. The book is filled with illustrations that show what clothing looked like in this century.

A Woman's Work is Never Done: Housework in the British Isles, 1650–1950. Davidson, Caroline (1982, Chatto & Windus, hardcover).

Insight into the lives of women, and a better understanding of how to wear the clothing when representing certain activities of the past.

Index